DOWN YONDER AT THE BACK END

Peggy E. Ellard

LARGE PRINT

Oxford

Copyright © Peggy E. Ellard, 2005

First published in Great Britain 2005
by
The Book Guild Ltd.

Published in Large Print 2007 by ISIS Publishing Ltd.,
7 Centremead, Osney Mead, Oxford OX2 0ES
by arrangement with
The Book Guild Ltd.

The moral right of the author has been asserted

British Library Cataloguing in Publication Data
Ellard, Peggy E.
    Down yonder at the back end. – Large print ed.
    (Isis reminiscence series)
    1. Ellard, Peggy E.
    2. Women – England – Biography
    3. Women – England – Social conditions – 20th
    century
    4. Large type books
    5. England – Social life and customs – 20th century
    6. England – Biography
    I. Title
    942'.082'092

ISBN 978–0–7531–9404–1 (hb)
ISBN 978–0–7531–9405–8 (pb)

Printed and bound in Great Britain by
T. J. International Ltd., Padstow, Cornwall

*This book is dedicated
to my family;
past, present and future*

1900

I am just reflecting on the attitudes, ignorance and secrecy that were around during the early part of the twentieth century and on my life from then to the present day. This account is a reflection on my part — first, hearsay, then my memories — of how life was.

My mother, Nellie, was born in 1901. She was very talented — very musical and with a good singing voice, something my twin brother Bill inherited. She was also artistic. Her paintings of flowers were hung on the school walls and when one day the School Governors visited and saw her work they suggested that Mother should be given special training. They would take her under their wings and help her to find work as a florist and also instruction in art. Unfortunately, her parents would not allow this as they needed her to go and earn money. She came from a big family and was one of 13 children. How different her life would have been — her talent most probably recognised — if she had been born in a different era.

Mother met Jack Holland, whom she married when she was still a teenager, at just 19 years old. She went to live with Jack and his family, but they were desperate for their own home. At that time they were living in the top floor flat of a three-storey house, with just a kitchen and one bedroom. The toilet was downstairs on the first floor, fresh water had to be collected from a tap halfway down the house and the slops had to be taken down to the ground floor to be emptied. Cooking and boiling nappies were done on a gas ring in the kitchen and the main wash was taken to the public baths once a week. Mother and Jack's first child, Jackie, was born after a year of marriage.

Jack was a chauffeur and his work often took him away from home for days at a time. He frequently had to drive his employer down to Worcester at weekends and it was there that he had an affair with one of the maids. Mum trusted him and not knowing the ways of men, was shocked when she eventually found out about Jack's adultery. In fact, she was devastated. It was at this time that George Brice came on the scene. Mother took solace with him and fell for his charms; then, hey presto, Bill and I were on our way into this world.

George was our biological father. He was born towards the end of 1899, the eldest child of a very large family. When he won a scholarship to attend the local grammar school his parents could not afford to buy the school uniform. Therefore, his uniform comprised of his grandmother's spring-side boots, with whatever other garments the family managed to obtain second-hand. Even his shirt collar had to be made out of cardboard. The humiliation of this was too much for him. He left within the first week and went to work as a window cleaner to earn money to help the family. This was still his job when he met Mother.

1924

When Bill and I were born, Mother and baby Jackie were still living with Jack Holland. Although the midwives who attended Mother at our birth knew she was expecting twins, they never told her — for some strange reason. It was no surprise to them, but Mother was in for a shock when two babies arrived in the early hours of the 17th August, 1924. We were six weeks premature. We weighed only approximately nine pounds between us. However, we were not treated like premature babies but were bathed as soon as we were born. So we did not settle happily in this world and screamed for hours on end. The doctor, on one of his visits, suggested throwing us out of the window — joking, of course! — but Mother was at her wits' end. She wrote to the Alexandra Nurses' Association. One of the nurses came to see her and recommended that the food we were being given was far too strong for our delicate digestions. Instead she suggested feeding us Nestlé's milk, and from that day we thrived. Well! That's until Jackie got the measles. We were nine months old at the time and both caught it. It turned to pneumonia and we were taken to Hackney Hospital and quickly christened, as we were not expected to live. We were named William and Peggy — though William was always known as Bill. Fortunately, we survived and were given the surname of Holland, Jack's surname, although he was not our biological father. On leaving hospital, Mother was given white cotton sleeveless jackets filled with cotton wool to keep us warm; the forerunners of the padded waistcoats which are popular today. These had to be washed regularly so Mother had to make a lot more.

After a while we were taken to live at Regent's Park with our real father, George. Jackie came too, but one day Jackie's father took him out for the day and he never returned to us — he had been taken to live with his grandparents and Jack. We saw him one more time: Mother took us to his school and we watched him through the school railings when it was his playtime. Mother talked to him and we returned home with her being very upset; I can still remember it very clearly. It was only when I was very much older that I was told he was my half-brother. I still have a school photo of him. Mother could not get help to have Jackie returned to her; in the eyes of the law, she was at fault.

I have never seen or heard of Jackie since. Mother never ever forgot him. She sent presents to him regularly on his birthday and at Christmas; whether he ever received them she never knew. She spoke to me about him a few days before she died — she always thought she would see him again, her firstborn! But she never did.

We lived in the basement of a Victorian house near Regent's Park. The house was rather gloomy, especially when the weather was foggy. Our flat was lit by gaslight and small oil lamps for the hall and the bedroom. Great care had to be taken with the mantles for both the gas fittings and the oil lamps because they shattered very easily. I often watched my father cleaning them and levelling the wicks. We also had a crystal set that my parents used to try to listen to. Bill and I often had the earphones placed on our ears to listen. Bill said he could hear properly and understood, but I never did. All I could hear was a scratching sound, very boring! That was, of course, the beginning of today's modern lifestyle of radios, hi-fi and computers. We lived next door to the piano factory and used to hear the pianos being tuned.

When the milkman called, Mother would go out to him with a jug. The milkman would sell her milk costing so much a gill. The copper measures were hung on the side of his handcart. There was always great excitement when the rag and bone man came round; if Mother had plenty of woollen or cotton things for him she could choose crockery from his cart. Otherwise we would have a goldfish, which of course was what we wanted, although they never lived long.

Bill and I were quite popular at school, especially after an incident at home that everyone knew about except us; we were kept very much in the dark about it. A neighbour met us from school that day and took us home, but did not tell us anything. We found that there was a commotion at home, with the police calling and all sorts. It seemed that the lady who lived upstairs, Miss Joyce, had committed suicide by throwing herself over the banister rail in our house. Miss Joyce had used to teach English to foreign students. She had been a very forbidding presence, very scary at times. Mother and Father were questioned by police at the local police station so when we arrived home from school that day we were told to go to bed and our tea would be brought to us. We had no idea what was going on at the time, so you see we were later told by other children what had happened. Naturally gory details were added. It was amazing how popular we became overnight, with people just wanting to know the ins and outs, but unfortunately for them we knew nothing!

About a year earlier than this incident, while Mother was out shopping, Bill and I had gone to Miss Joyce's apartment and ate a whole hand of bananas that were in her fruit dish. We left only the skins behind. When we were having our supper that evening she came down to our flat and said, "NELLIE! Look what I have found!" She was holding up the empty banana skins. We were in so much trouble; we had always been forbidden to go into Miss Joyce's rooms. Also, Mother had to go and buy more bananas, which she could ill afford. Our poor tummies revolted during that night and we had no sympathy from our parents. I don't know why we did this, because we were terrified of Miss Joyce! How we had the courage to go into her rooms I will never know. Maybe the thrill of being naughty appealed to us.

The lady who lived next door had a parrot and would put him out in his cage on the front balcony on sunny days. Bill, myself and local friends used to have great fun asking the parrot the time and he in turn used to swear at us in no uncertain terms. We also enjoyed playing on the ice cart (there were no fridges in those days) when it came to deliver ice to the fishmonger's and the butcher's. While the driver was delivering his huge block of ice, which he would balance on a sack and carry on his shoulder, we kids used to scramble onto the cart to find some chippings of ice, hoping to take some home. Of course it always melted before we got back home. Often we were on the cart when it moved off. We would slither on to the rail at the back of the cart and hang on for dear life while enjoying a free ride. Many times we were told not to do this. It was dangerous. While we were outside the butcher's shop, we also found it interesting to watch him make sausages. He had the sausage machine in his shop window and we found the sight of the sausages whizzing out of the machine very funny.

During the school holidays we would be given free tickets to visit the London Zoo, as we lived close by; often we would hear the animals at night, especially the lions roaring. Armed with sandwiches and a drink, we would have an enjoyable day. We used to play dare, seeing which of us could stay in the polecats' house the longest: it used to stink. Also we enjoyed watching children having elephant rides. It was fun watching the elephants having drinks of water, as sometimes they would spray it all over people queuing for their rides. We knew this would happen so we would stand clear and watch the others get soaked. It was great fun. The camel rides were very popular too. On our way to the zoo we used to watch the dray horses pulling the barges along the Regent's Canal and often in summer we used to see adults and children swimming in it, but we couldn't swim. Some children used to jump on the backs of the barges for free rides but we never did: our parents had always given us dire warnings about strangers.

We were also warned to be careful of the barrel-organ grinder. He had a monkey and there were always dancers very colourfully dressed. We would follow them from street to street. Our parents warned us that these were dangerous people but we still used to follow. We felt frightened but the magic of the organ and the dancers just compelled us to follow them.

One day, when my mother was late meeting us from school, we decided to run away. We were only five years old at the time. I can remember walking along Park Street towards Camden Town when a policeman came along and took us to a police station; I believe it was the one on Albany Road. I cried all the way there. We were told to sit down on the floor and given a cup of cocoa and then I made my brother ashamed of me because I wet the floor. Eventually our father found us, after visiting various police stations. He carried us home, one on his shoulders and one in his arms. When we finally arrived home, our house was full of people. It seemed they had all been searching Primrose Hill. My mother sobbed as she hugged us.

Another incident I remember is the time when Bill and I had been to Sunday School and during the following week were playing in Regent's Park. We were walking round the boating lake when Bill said, "See if you can walk on the water like Jesus." I tried, immediately sank and was hauled out of the water on an oar by somebody who was out boating. I then had to walk home all through the park, dripping wet. I had a jacket wrapped around my shoulders and Bill was trotting along beside me, very shamefaced. I enjoyed the attention I received from neighbours who brought me sweeties because I had had such a bad experience! Bill was not impressed that I got the attention and sweeties when it had all been his idea.

One day while out with my parents, we were walking along Park Street towards Camden Town when Father pointed out a strange-looking man, who was sparsely dressed — I thought it was a sheet he was wearing. He was so thin. We were told he was Mahatma Gandhi. Whenever his name is mentioned on the news or in films, that memory comes back to me.

One day at school we had a lesson that involved threading beads onto cotton. One boy put a bead up his nostril but fortunately the teacher managed to remove it for him. I had copied him and felt such a fool, especially when I tried to remove it myself and just pushed it higher. I never mentioned this to a soul. Eventually I began to cry whenever Mother washed my face. Mother used to listen to me when I was asleep and would hear this strange whistling noise coming from my nostril as I breathed. I was taken to a specialist who said there was a foreign body in my nose; I would have to have my tonsils and adenoids removed to find

10

out what was causing this. I was asked various questions but in no way would I confess to what I had done. Even after the operation when the bead was found, I still denied all knowledge of it.

We always enjoyed May 24th, Empire Day. We would go to school dressed in red, white and blue clothes and carry a small Union Jack. During assembly we would parade round the school hall and sing "Jerusalem", "God Save the King" and other patriotic songs. (Of course, we did not sing "There'll always be an England" because it hadn't been written back then.) We then had the afternoon off and that was also exciting.

We began to get new residents living in the upstairs rooms. My parents became very good friends with Jack on the top floor; Mother even looked after him when he had flu. Soon after this, things began to change at home — for one thing, there were quarrels between our parents. Auntie Ivy came to live with us at about that time and her friend Len always bought shrimps and winkles for Sunday tea. Auntie Elsie, Uncle Ronnie, Auntie Winnie and Uncle Fred also visited very often. They always used to take Bill and me out.

We used to go and play with a boy named Geoffrey who lived across the road. He had a nanny to look after him instead of his parents and I always felt sorry for him because of this. His nanny was very strict; he was made to stand in the corner of the room at the slightest misdemeanour. The nanny often took us to play with children who also had that sort of life; I always vowed to myself I would not leave my children in the care of strangers. Most mornings these nannies would take their charges for a walk across Primrose Hill or Regent's Park, all gossiping about the mothers. We often went with them and had to walk very sedately and not giggle, which we found extremely hard to do. Geoffrey's mother was presented at Court, which was quite something in those days. We and the neighbours watched while her photo was taken on her doorstep before being driven off to Buckingham Palace. I remember she was all dressed up with ostrich feathers on. Poor Geoffrey was left out of all this excitement. I expect he had committed some minor offence.

One afternoon when we were in Regent's Park with our Uncle Fred, we saw the airship R101 going across to France on its maiden voyage. Uncle and Bill were very impressed but I was not. Later we heard that there had been a terrible disaster; the airship had crashed soon after it crossed over the channel. We all went to Mornington Crescent Railway Station and watched the train pass through, bearing back to Bedfordshire all the flower-draped coffins. It was very sad.

Our neighbour Mrs Timms took Bill and me to Selfridges one day to see Amelia Earhart; she was there in the foyer with her little red plane. I had no idea then of her great achievement and could not see what the fuss was all about. I am now pleased that I went and of course now realise just how brave she was.

I was a nervous child and used to stutter and blink my eyelids a lot and when Bill was about 12 he developed a nervous twitch. Whether this was due to us being twins or to our home life I will never know. We both grew out of it but we were teased mercilessly at school. I do know that the next episode in our lives affected Bill very much. He told me all his innermost feelings shortly before he died.

1933

One afternoon my mother packed a bag and took me away from home. I never even said goodbye to Bill, my father or my aunt. I remember it was a damp day and it seemed a long while waiting for a coach. I think we waited in either Aldgate or Leadenhall Street. I can see, even now, the model liners in shipping office windows there. Eventually we boarded a coach that took us to Romford. We stayed in rented accommodation for a couple of weeks and when I enquired about Bill I was told Mother would go and get him later. We moved to a newly-built house in Hornchurch, so different from the Victorian house I was used to. Bill duly came to live with us. We were then told that Jack, the man from the upstairs flat, was our new father. Our surname would now be Berkley, we were to call him Dad and on no account were we to tell a soul what had happened, not even at school. When I last saw Bill, before he died, he told me how utterly rejected he felt when Mother took me away without him. He had always been Mother's favourite, you see. He was brought to our new home to find he had a new father, with Mother giving her affections to him instead! Bill told me that feeling of rejection never left him. I suppose being female, I found it easier to accept my new father. He was a very kind man, but boys often cannot get on with their own fathers. So accepting an unfamiliar man as his father must have been very difficult for Bill.

Our lives changed so much. We did not have much opportunity to chat at our new home; we were never allowed to go back into our bedrooms once we had come down in the mornings. Then Bill would be off with his friends and I was usually helping my mother, so we did not really play and talk as much as we used to. We never discussed our new life but just accepted it. I realise now what a culture shock it must have been for us. This was a new housing estate and we had to play on the waste ground which was rapidly being built upon. The children on the estate were mainly from the Manchester area and their fathers worked at the new Ford works at Dagenham. There were also the children of the Irish navvies who were building the new houses. I thought these children were foreigners, because their language was so strange. One child asked me, "Are you a pro dog or cat lick?" I had to ask mother what the answer was; it turned out I was a pro dog (a Protestant). I was used to playing with the Jewish children at school. They were allowed to wait in the classroom while we had prayers each morning. I used to wish I was Jewish so I could miss prayers. My new classmates, the Mancunians and Irish, I found more difficult to get used to.

One afternoon our father came to visit. We were sent out to play and while we were out playing we saw him

15

leaving in a taxi. I never saw him again. I now know Bill contacted him during the war. I had the chance to see him again, but I stupidly declined; I must admit I have since regretted it.

A few months later there was a new arrival in the family — my sister Sylvia was born. We were at Sunday School when she arrived; a neighbour met us afterwards and we went and had our tea at her house. What a surprise we had when we got home and saw this new baby. I loved her dearly and still do, but I must confess to feeling jealous at times. It was not explained to us who Sylvia's real father was and I often think we must have been very naïve not to ask questions. Perhaps it was because we had been told not to say anything about our previous life when we first moved to Hornchurch. Or perhaps we just thought it was none of our business.

I did not get on very well at my new school in Rainsford Way. I was too much of a chatterbox. My teacher made a red cardboard tongue which was hung round my neck. I suppose it was about six inches long. I had to wear it all day, even to go out in the playground at playtime. Still I chatted. A longer tongue was made for me. Still I chatted, until it was decided I should be caned. First I had to stand outside the headmaster's room and have my name entered in the black book, and then I had to stand and receive the cane on both hands in front of the whole school in assembly. Then one day when our teacher had to leave the room for a minute she put one of the boys in my class in charge. This boy told me to stop talking, although I hadn't been. When our teacher returned she asked had anyone been talking and he said I had. So! I was immediately sent to the headmaster. I was furious — I had accepted punishment when I had done wrong, but this time I had not! This was too much. So, I crept out of school. It was quite difficult because I had to crawl under the windows of various classrooms so as not to be seen. I ran all the way home, sobbing. On my arrival home my mother was very cross with me. "I expect you deserved it," she said. I refused to go back to school. After much discussion with my brother — we were in the same class, so he had seen everything — it was decided that I was in the right. My mother wrote to the school authorities and I have no idea what transpired: as usual, we were kept in the dark. I eventually returned to school. I was never punished again.

Needless to say, I did not pass the scholarship exam and neither did Bill. We went to different senior schools. Bill got on very well, but I just played about. I wanted the girls to like me. I knew the teachers would not, as my reputation came with me.

September 1935

One day around this time I came home from school to find that some sort of celebration had taken place. Uncle Johnny and Aunt Rose were there. My little sister had on a pretty pale green dress, which an aunt had made for her. I have since concluded that this must have been the day my mother married our new dad. The following March, my brother John was born. Dad was taken ill at that time with erysipelas; he had to go to an isolation hospital. As he had brought the office keys home with him, Mother sent me to London to his office at Friar's House in New Broad Street to take them back. I was told to speak only to a commissionaire who would help me find Dad's office. Mother was surprised how quickly I arrived back home. That was when I became general runabout.

Bill and I used to have to take turns in getting the battery recharged for our radio, which involved carrying the battery to a local radio shop. When it was ready we had to carry it home with strict instructions not to tip it up. It was a long way to walk, trying to keep the battery steady.

I used to be sent to a café that had a sign saying "You may telephone from here" to enquire about my father's progress in the isolation hospital. He was not allowed any visitors, but often after school I would have to go to the hospital, pushing the little ones in their pram, to take to Dad whatever he required. Soon after my father came home from the hospital, Bill came down with scarlet fever, so he was sent there too. And a few months after Bill came home, Sylvia got diphtheria. Because we shared the same bed and I had eaten part of her boiled egg at breakfast it was assumed that I would definitely come down with it too, so Bill and I were not allowed to go to school for three weeks. I did not get ill, though, and neither did Bill. In my mind I feel it was partly because I had a huge appetite and was always hungry. Mother was a good cook and food was plentiful, so I was well nourished.

Father kept an allotment and grew all our vegetables, while Mother kept hens (cooking the potato peelings for the hens used to smell awful, but it was necessary for the eggs, and they had to be fed before dusk each day), as well as a cockerel who provided our Christmas dinner. We also kept rabbits; John was upset when his pet ran away!! I used to spend a great deal of time minding my sister when she was crawling and learning to walk in the garden and I would eat all the available nasturtium leaves and seeds — and most likely plenty of black fly along with them. I have often wondered how many I consumed! When I was out walking with the children I used to pick all the berries off the bushes as I walked along and I would eat pocketfuls. I think all this must have given me an immunity to the various illnesses present at the time.

Weekends were always the same. I would push John and Sylvia in the bassinet pram to Romford market to buy the weekend's food — usually a piece of beef or bacon and some veg. If any shopping was unsuitable I would be sent back with it, so I really did try to get it right first time. On Sunday mornings I used to take the kids out, come rain, hail or shine. They used to like to feed the ducks, especially when the lake was frozen and they could watch the ducks skidding towards us for the bread. Occasionally Bill would come with us and then we would take a different route to Raphael's Park. It would involve dragging the pram with the children in it over an iron bridge, which passed over the main train lines to Liverpool Street Station. John and Sylvia used to love that and they enjoyed even more the bumpity-bump ride down the stairs on the other side.

When we arrived home after our long walk, dinner was usually ready, but if not, I was sent out again until it was. Then Mother would put John and Sylvia's meal out first and I would feed them. I must confess I ate more than they did. It would be one spoonful for them — they were slow eaters — and two for me. Mother used to say the fresh air did them the world of good, when I took their empty plates out to the kitchen.

I was a Girl Guide and in 1937 I went to guide camp in Ingatestone, along with my friend Gladys. Each patrol had their own bell tent and with instructions from our patrol leader we had to help erect it. We had to bring a palliasse with us, which we would take to a barn and fill with straw. This was to be our mattress. We had great fun filling it, but Gladys and I were greedy and put far too much straw in ours. We just kept rolling off it on that first night. First thing the next morning we went and emptied most of it out. We also made shoe racks to keep our shoes off the damp ground, coat hangers for our clothes and a sort of tripod to hold a wash basin, all of which were good practice for all the knots and suchlike that we had learnt. There was an inspection of the tent each morning by the captain and points were given each day. Each patrol had various tasks to perform every day, but Gladys and I used to hide up a cedar tree and watch everyone else working until we smelt the food was ready. But we did not get away with it. For punishment we had to keep the big dustbin filled with fresh water — it was a brand new one kept for that purpose. We had to take water cans to the far end of the field to fill them and then replenish the bin. Between us we decided that it would be far simpler to take the bin to the water supply — we had not reckoned on not being able to lift the darn thing when it was full! We had to tip some out before we could drag it back. Despite all this, I enjoyed that week very much, sitting around the campfire singing songs.

1938

I worked hard during my last term at school and got an A in almost every subject. The headmistress called me to her room and asked me, "Why have you not worked like this throughout?" I just said, "Well, I need a reference ready for going to work." I started work on my 14th birthday. On leaving school in July we were given our reports and also a green card which we had to take to the City of London, to a labour exchange called Snow Hill, near the Bank of England. I went there with my friend Gladys. They did not have any office vacancies for us there but suggested we should try the Shoreditch labour exchange and told us how to get there. Needless to say, we had to go by shanks's pony. After walking for what seemed like an eternity all through the East End we finally arrived in Shoreditch, only to be told that there was a job for one person only in an office in City Road. Although there was only one job we were told we should both go along and see. So we trudged to City Road and found the office. A very nice lady called Miss Winch interviewed us. She took one look at my report and said, "You cannot stay away like this when you come to work." It seems I had been away from school 29 times (if my little sister was being difficult I was kept at home to look after her). In the end Miss Winch said she would employ both Gladys and me, and we had to start the following day — Wednesday, 17th August, 1938. We were told we would receive 15 shillings a week and one day holiday the first year. We were so pleased we had got a job that we didn't think to find out the name of the firm we were going to work for. We didn't even know the exact address. We had almost got to Liverpool Street Station on our way home when we realised this, and we had to go all the way back to City Road to find out. The firm was called Chain Store Finance Trust Co., City Road.

We arrived home extremely tired after our long walk and it didn't seem long at all before we were back at City Road again the next morning, this time to start work, myself wearing second-hand private school uniform of blue gingham dress and blazer. I hated this; Mother thought it looked smart. We had to catch the workman's train to qualify for the cheap ticket and that meant we had to be at Liverpool Street Station by eight o'clock each morning. We would spend the next hour strolling through the back streets towards City Road, past all the tenements and slum areas. One road was called Worship Street; the tenants of the flats along it were on strike against the landlords, refusing to pay their rents. The banners and slogans strung across the tenements we found quite shocking. We never realised such homes existed.

When the weather was colder we used to find bakers' shops and stand over the grids on the street where

23

warm air was released, until the office was opened. Our boss, Mr Peck, used to insist that all the windows were opened wide during our lunch hour, so often it seemed warmer to go out. I enjoyed having snowball fights in Bunhill Row Cemetery during winter; in summer we'd go there to eat our sandwiches. We were still kids at heart and did not realise we were on a sacred burial ground. Sometimes we would go to Whitecross Street where there was a market. One stallholder had snakes crawling around on his stall, and some girls let him put them round their necks. I would not; I could not even bring myself to touch one. We used to buy lovely coconut brittle there, though: four ounces for a penny.

One day Miss Winch sent me to Kingsway to fetch carbon paper from a firm called Gestetner. I had to catch a tram from Old Street and had quite a fright when it went underground — Miss Winch had not thought to warn me! When I got there, the building was huge. I was standing by the lift, worrying about going into it, when a commissionaire came along and helped me. He even put me on the right tram for going back to Old Street.

I was taught how to use the Burroughs adding machine and I enjoyed that work. If we were fed up with working we could make the machine add incorrectly by resting our hand on the motor bar when we pressed in the numbers. The total was usually wrong by about five shillings and the engineer would be sent for. We were all in love with him! We could not do this too often, of course.

When summer came, Gladys and I were given our one-day holiday. We spent it walking to the Southend Arterial Road and sitting watching the cars go by. I was given one shilling pocket money a week at that time; the remainder of my wages went on fares and towards the family budget. In those days my mother used to make me wear a corset, a horrible thing; I was not allowed to wear a bra. Mother said only street women wore those things. I had no idea what a street woman was and I dared not ask. Bras did not enter my life until after I was married.

1939

In 1939 we moved to a new house in Hornchurch and there I met Fred. He was a neighbour's son and used to call for me to go out for the evening. Usually he had to wait because I would be upstairs getting John and Sylvia to sleep, although John was always very good and fell asleep easily. Often I would doze off myself and Mother would come and wake me if Fred was waiting downstairs, but if not I was left until morning. I did on occasions pinch Sylvia if I wanted to go out in a hurry — of course, it didn't help, but I felt better for it!

The two of us used to go out along with Fred's friend Ted and his girlfriend, Winnie. I did not like Ted very much in those days. We used to go roller-skating — well, the other three did; I couldn't even keep my balance on the coconut matting that we walked on to get to the rink. I usually spent the evening on my bottom. Fred and Ted tried holding me up and taking me round the rink but I would always be black and blue with bruises the next day. I'm not a sporty type.

September 1939 — War is Declared

Fred was called up and went into the navy. Ted at that time joined the Home Guard, but was eventually called up too and went into the RAF.

Dad was keen for me to learn shorthand but I was hopeless at it. I always hated having to learn English at school, so any career which involved words or spelling did not appeal to me. I am sorry now that I did not pay attention to that subject. I left my first job with the Chain Store Finance Co. and went to work for Thomas de la Rue, a firm that printed banknotes. We had to start at eight o'clock in the morning and if we were late the doors would be closed. We would then have to wait outside for 15 minutes and lose 15 minutes' pay.

Mother never told me about the facts of life. What a fright I had when my periods started! Mother just said not to tell Father or my brothers — it was another secret I had to keep. When I started going out with Fred, she told me, "Don't bring any trouble home, you know what will happen to you," but I had no idea what she was on about. I soon learnt about the ways of life by listening to the girls I was now working with. They were naughty, but felt they wanted to give the lads a good time, because they were going away to fight. Sexual freedom did not start in the sixties; the war started it, albeit hush hush. I was still at Thomas de la Rue when the Blitz began and Bill was at that time working for Cable and Wireless as a messenger boy.

We moved from Hornchurch to Seven Kings, quite close to Barkingside. It was near the River Thames and the London docks so we were really and truly blitzed. We would spend the nights, when the raids were on, sitting in the hall cupboard. Mother put a mattress on the floor for Sylvia and John. Bill and I would sit with the gas and electric meters at our backs. We still went off to work each morning in the city. One Saturday afternoon we watched a dogfight between our Spitfires and a German aircraft. We saw the German airman parachuting down to earth and ran to where we thought he had landed, but we were too late. It was all over by the time we got there.

Where I worked it was the custom for news to be announced over the tannoy each day. If a member of staff was bombed or a relative in the forces killed or injured, you could collect flowers to take to the bereaved family or the injured person. I used to wish something would happen in my family so I could take the flowers home — I feel ashamed of myself now for thinking like that, but at 16 I did not realise the horrors of war. It was just an adventure to me.

While my parents were on a visit to Auntie Ivy (mother's sister), who was living in north London, the air-raid siren sounded. Ivy said I must go to the underground station at Finsbury Park, or I would lose my place in the shelter. Father said, "Come on, Nell, we are going home, we won't stay here on our own." (Although Danko the Alsatian dog was sitting comfortably in his kennel.) They arrived home to Seven Kings travelling with the noise of ack-ack fire from the guns situated in Finsbury Park and Clissold Park and the searchlights. That night Ivy's house was bombed. Danko was found a few days later, alive. He came crawling out of the rubble when he heard Ivy's voice and was taken to my grandparents' home to be looked after, much to the displeasure of the various moggies who also had taken up residence with them. Ivy managed to salvage a few bits and pieces of her home and then rented two rooms near Grandma. I went to help Ivy sort out her bits and pieces. We found broken plates, chipped or cracked cups, then we found a cup, whole, not a crack in it anywhere, *then I dropped it.* Words cannot express just how I felt, especially as Ivy, seeing that, just broke down and wept. She sobbed uncontrollably for about 20 minutes. She had been very brave coping on her own. Her husband was stationed in Syria with the Royal Engineers. He was given compassionate leave. It took a few weeks before he finally arrived home,

I visited Ivy each week after that as I was working in the City. I used to wait in my grandparents' house for Ivy to come home from work, so I experienced Grandma going off to work. Grandma loved doing her bit for the war effort. She worked 6.00p.m. until

10.00p.m. at Cossors Radio Factory in Highbury. After bearing 13 children and being virtually housebound, this freedom was wonderful to her. Granddad would sit by the fire and nag her, "Don't forget your cup, your sandwich, and torch", then he'd say, "Hurry up, woman, you'll be late". One evening she was late home. "Where have you been, woman?" he said. "I was helping an old lady home," she replied. Grandma must have been well into her 70s.

One evening while I was travelling home from work with a colleague an air raid started. It was a very slow journey, with the train stopping for long intervals. When we reached Manor Park Station most of the passengers decided to leave the train but we stayed on. However, after another crawl for about half a mile the train stopped again and by then we'd also had enough. We decided we would walk along the track to Ilford Station. Well! I climbed out of the train and didn't realise just how far down it was to the track. My colleague threw down our handbags, umbrellas and music cases — it was the fashion in those days to use music cases to carry sandwiches, books and other necessary items. She started to climb down too but the train started to move off so she had to climb back up. The sight of her clambering back up in the dim light of the searchlights struck me as very funny. I couldn't stop laughing. I picked up all our belongings — handbags, music cases, umbrellas and the evening papers. I could only see between the searchlights so it was quite difficult. Well, I walked past the new flyover which was being constructed then — with great difficulty because

30

of the heaps of sand and bags of cement — and I only had the searchlights to guide me. I could not stop laughing — it seems my colleague and other passengers standing on Ilford Station could hear me coming along the track long before they could see me, I was laughing so much. When I arrived home Mother did not think it was very funny. I couldn't tell her what had happened for giggling. In fact, every time I think about it, even now, I burst out laughing. Of course what I did was extremely dangerous, but teenagers never see danger.

A few nights later our house was shattered. It wasn't a direct hit but we lost windows, doors and the ceiling of one bedroom. Mother heard from her parents that an uncle living in Lincolnshire knew of a cottage in Bratoft, about a mile from where he lived, which was available for five shillings a week rent. Its name was Moat Cottage. Mother and Father decided to take the family there and they had all the furniture sent up. Bill went with them, but I stayed behind to look after the cat, among other things. I soon learnt how quickly food goes off if not dealt with properly. I am surprised the cat survived the awful minced steak I cooked for him — there was no tinned food for pets in those days. Dad came back after a week in Lincolnshire, and then I had to go up there because Sylvia would not settle, especially at bedtime. She was used to me putting her to bed, you see. My Uncle Will and Aunt Dolly lived in a tied cottage, belonging to the railway; his duties were to open the gates on the crossing to allow the trains through, then to close them again so that cars could continue their journeys. They had a good life there and when trains came down from Grimsby to London the drivers would often throw fish to my uncle. When he was short of coal he would show a piece of it to a passing train driver and they would shovel a fair amount down to him. My uncle and aunt never visited us in our cottage because he had to be on call 24 hours a day, and Aunt Dolly had to be there too, just in case. That railway line was eventually closed down by Dr Beeching.

We were known as refugees from London and were quite a novelty to the locals. Evacuees were not usually sent there and we were the first they had seen. I think they were quite surprised we were not flea-ridden! Word about us soon got around and a doctor from the next village — Burgh le Marsh — thought I would make a good skivvy for his wife. He called at our cottage and asked Mother if I would like a job. He took me back to his home and his wife interviewed me. She told me I would have to look after three children and help in the home. They had soldiers billeted in their basement and I was told not to fraternise with them. After the interview she said I could go home and come to start work on the following Monday. She closed the door immediately behind me and never gave me any indication of how I was supposed to get home. I started walking but then got to a crossroads where I stood absolutely petrified as to which road to take — there were no signposts in those days. I was crying there when the baker's boy came along in his bakery van, and he took me home. His name was Arnold Hansom, but I called him Handsome Arnold. Mother was absolutely furious at the way I had been treated and refused to let me work for them, much to my relief. A few months later I was walking with Sylvia and John in a field close to the railway line when we saw a train on its way to Grimsby being machine-gunned by a German plane. We could see the pilot easily, doing his dirty deed. He dropped a couple of bombs too, on the village where the doctor lived. There was quite a bit of damage and a few casualties. This was their first taste of war and it was totally unexpected there, in the heart of the country. I wondered what the doctor and his wife thought about that.

Among all the belongings Dad had brought up from London was an Aladdin oil lamp that we had to use for lighting. Drinking water came from the pump at the front of the cottage and for washing water we had to drop a bucket on a rope down the well. There was a trapdoor over it for safety. Our toilet was situated down the garden; Bill painted the name "Berchtesgaden", Hitler's country residence, on the door. The toilet consisted of a bucket with a seat over it. The bucket had to be emptied every day into a deep hole that Dad dug at the bottom of the garden. Every time the bucket was emptied, a shovel of earth was thrown on top. I soon discovered the best place to stand when there was a gale blowing while emptying that bucket! During winter, bucket and seat were kept in the back washhouse, which contained the copper in the corner. That had to be lit underneath to heat the water to wash and boil the clothes. We also had a huge mangle with big wooden rollers and it took a while for me to get used to turning it. Cooking was difficult over the open fire. Saucepans had to be balanced directly on the hot coals and if the coals shifted as they burnt through the saucepans would tip over. So they had to be watched, all the time. The oven was also very temperamental — if the weather was sluggish then the fire would not burn bright and many a time have I pushed the hot coals under the oven hoping to get a meal cooked.

We used to have sticky flypapers hanging in various positions around the cottage to trap the flying insects — ugh! Often my hair used to get stuck to one, the cottage having low ceilings.

Occasionally villagers would call round for the evening. Mother would play the piano and sing music-hall songs. Bill would stand on the table and sing songs like "Because", "Trees", and "O Sol a Mio", which were very popular at the time. Mother also spent many hours crying. My cousin once said to her, "Nellie, why do you not cry over the copper? It will then be filled ready for the washing!"

Sylvia went to the village school, which had one classroom and one teacher for all the pupils. John went too when he was a little older. Their schooling was very poor, but they soon improved when we came back to London and eventually passed to go to grammar schools.

One day Mother took us to Skegness and while we were there we watched the raw recruits being trained ready to go into the Navy — how to march, rifle drill and all that. They must have felt embarrassed with civilians just standing watching them. A few yards of barbed wire had been cut away to allow civilians onto the beach, so they could enjoy themselves. While we were there, something happened that I will always remember. One of our bombers was coming back after a raid on Germany. He circled the area and plunged into the sea, probably about 50 yards from the shore. A number of men rushed to the children's boating lake and tried to row a small boat out to the plane but they were too late. I think of that tragic incident very often, especially on Armistice Day. It was so very sad. We all felt so helpless.

Later that day we were strolling around Woolworth's when a Norwegian sailor gave Mother two half-crowns to spend on John and Sylvia. She tried to converse with him and from what we could understand it seemed he had children in Norway and had not seen them in years.

One day Mother decided to pop back to London. I thought she would only be away a couple of days but in fact she stayed a week. She was very cross with me when she came home to find I had not done the week's wash. It was piled up in the scullery. I didn't know I had to do it. I had domestic science lessons at school, but was only taught how to wash and boil one article. When it came to a family wash I had not a clue! But I soon learnt as the weeks went by.

As winter approached, cans of drinking water had to be drawn every afternoon, because more often than not the pump would be frozen in the morning. The well water for washing was also collected in the afternoons and kept in buckets in the scullery. I was able to cope with all that, but ironing was a nightmare. I had to heat the flat iron on the red-hot coals and getting those coals hot was quite a problem at times. When the iron was hot I would have to rub it on an old sheet to remove the soot and by the time I had done that the darn thing was cold again. Washing up was done on the dining table with a tray to catch the drips. It was a messy business, especially as Mother insisted that the soot be removed from the pans each time I washed up.

Mother went to London again and this time stayed. She got herself a job there and lived with Dad in the air-raid shelter of his office.

Bill had a job on a farm. He used to come home filthy and would never change his clothes; he never ever liked washing. Mum often used to have to undress him after he went to bed. He would put on a clean vest over his dirty one. He loathed having to change his clothes — the cold, clean feel of them did not appeal to him. So it was not easy for me, trying to keep him clean without Mother there. He often used to go ratting with the farmers' sons. They were paid so much for each rat's tail, I cannot remember how much. But I do know he used to tease me with them and chase us all round the garden, with three of us screaming. The only way I could get my own back was when I'd say, "Pipe down, young 'un, I'm older than you." He never liked me being older than him, even if it was only by five minutes! But despite all that we were really very close and fond of each other.

Bill joined the Home Guard: "Dad's Army". He falsified his age to get in; he loved going out on manoeuvres at weekends.

One weekend when Mum and Dad came for the weekend Bill had a quarrel with them. He packed his bags and said he was going to leave home, but in the end he was persuaded to return to London with them. They all lived in the basement of Friar's House. Bill got his old job back with the Cable and Wireless. He also joined the City of London Home Guard. Dad used to have to do fire duty each night. He was on duty when all around St Paul's Cathedral was devastated; the building opposite his had a direct hit. Incendiary bombs were dropping everywhere. Bill was very useful up on the city office roof helping to put them out. While all this activity was going on I was looking after John and Sylvia in the comparative peace of the countryside.

Sheep used to graze in the field beside our cottage and during the night they would keep shuffling round to get to the warmth that emanated from it. They used to cough quite a lot and at first it was quite frightening — they sounded just like old men — but we got used to it.

Fortunately for me, when I was very young we had gaslights and I was used to the mantles being easily shattered. So when I had to fill the Aladdin lamp with paraffin each day and trim the wick when it became uneven, I knew I had to take great care with the mantle. On winter days the lamp had to be lit quite early so that the glass could warm up before it was turned up for full light. If I broke a mantle I had to go to Spilsby, five miles away, for another. Our local village store did not stock them. How the villagers managed I do not know. I suppose they must have got the bus to Spilsby like me. There was one bus there in the morning and one back in the afternoon and that was all. Rather than waiting till the afternoon I used to walk back. I didn't mind but the first time I did it I got a fright — I have always been scared of dogs and I was passing a farm when a dog rushed out, barking away. I was happily munching a bun at the time, so I threw it at him and while he was searching for it I just ran hell for leather. After that I used to arm myself with buns ready for my walk home. Sometimes Handsome Arnold would be on his baker's round and he would give me a lift. One day while I was waiting for the bus to Spilsby a car pulled up and I was offered a lift there. Despite being frightened, I accepted and the driver and I started chatting. He asked how long I had lived in that area and I started boasting about my husband and children, thinking I would be safe if he knew I had a family. Well, I felt an utter fool a few days later when I visited our neighbour's farm and discovered that the fellow who had given me a lift was the local vet, who obviously knew all about me. I ran and hid in a barn until he left: I didn't want him to see me, I felt so stupid.

I often think of things that seemed quite worrying at the time, but I never really had any cause for concern. Once I was alone in the cottage and I happened to notice a soldier coming across the field opposite. He knocked at the door but I was too frightened to answer.

When I finally looked outside I found a big bunch of honeysuckle he had left for me. The following weekend my parents came home and Dad was digging a new hole for me to use when needed, when who should come across the field but this fellow with some friends. Dad spoke to them and I never saw them again, thank goodness.

As the name of our cottage suggests, we had a moat on the right side and cows used to graze on the land encircled by the moat. We had a very hot summer that year so the moat dried up; walking down to the loo after dark was quite eerie then, as the cows could come across into our garden and I sometimes felt they were walking alongside me in the moonlight. I was busy indoors one day when I noticed the cows in our back garden — they had had the cheek to eat all my lovely tomatoes, which were just turning that beautiful orange colour before going red. I was so upset. That evening when we were having tea, the bull came and looked in the window. There was a pot of strawberry jam on the table and we got worried because it was coloured red. John, Sylvia and I all ended up under the table, hiding the jam in case the red made the bull stampede. Not that there was much room for that!

I had been finding it easier to use the pump water for all our needs and as the summer was so hot it eventually ran dry. After that I had to go to the neighbours for fresh water.

One day a flock of geese and the gander decided to visit us. The gander hissed and went for John and Sylvia so I had to chase him out of the garden using the yard broom. He got his leg caught on some barbed wire and was getting frantic. I don't know who was the more scared, that gander or me. I got the barbed wire off him and those geese never came back. I wonder why?

Our cottage was situated about 130 yards off the road and our path to the road was called the gatrum, in local dialect. One day Jim and John Garfett, the sons of the farmer who owned the field opposite our cottage, came down the gatrum leading two cows. They led one through the gate to the pasture where the bull was grazing. The bull ignored her — he was only interested in the cow on the outside and she liked him too. The cow inside the pasture was just grazing merrily without a care in the world and John and Jim were beginning to get quite angry. I, not being a country lass and not knowing much about the birds and the bees or indeed the farm animals, was finding the whole saga quite amusing. The bull got annoyed when they kept trying to get him to mate with that cow and in the end he charged at Jim. Jim ran away and tried to clear the hedge and luckily his father, Mr Garfett, happened to be passing on his way to collect the cows for milking. He and John were able to get Jim to safety.

I always called my cat in at night. One night when I went to call her the wretched cat would not come in. With much struggling I carried "her" in, only to discover I had an identical cat sitting peacefully indoors. Then all hell was let loose, plus fur and caterwauling. We managed to get that other cat out, but I have since felt sorry for him. He probably thought he was in luck!

Only Handsome Arnold the baker ever came down to our cottage. Our milk ration was left at the bottom of the gatrum. The farmer had to send the full quota of milk each day to the Milk Marketing Board and should there be a shortfall we would have to go without. On Thursdays the butcher came; he would sound his horn and I would run up the gatrum to his van with a large plate to collect our meat ration for the week. It was not much for one adult and two children — usually only corned beef and perhaps a couple of chops. He would also bring me big beef bones which I would boil and then add vegetables to; I can still taste and feel in my mouth the awful glutinous soup which I made. The only other alternative was a scrap of cheese with red cabbage, but we survived well on this diet.

One morning I received a letter from Mother telling me that a coalman would be delivering a ton of coal that day — country people are wise enough to get their winter's supply of coal in the summer and we had not yet been able to. There had been some coal in the barn when we arrived but it did not last long with cooking, even in the summer. Well! When I saw this old man dragging his horse — which did not look like it would be able to pull an empty cart, let alone one full of coal — I was a bit concerned. It got worse when I discovered that the coal was loose in the cart and I would have to help unload it. All I had to carry the coal in was one small bucket and a hand basin. The coalman could not get the cart near the barn because of the moat, so there I was, toing and froing. Now at that time Sylvia was subject to bilious attacks (nothing to do with my dreadful soups, I might add). I was instructed that we should all have "opening medicine" once a week. For me this was either syrup of figs or senna pods soaked overnight to infuse into a sort of tea; for John and Sylvia it was Milk of Magnesia. On the evening before the coalman arrived I duly gave the children their opening medicine. I was still ferrying the coal to the barn when John appeared on the step to announce he had the runs! I wished at that moment I could have run miles and miles away. I never gave either of the children opening medicine again. What a peculiar custom it was.

But despite all the aggravations, I was happy living this life, strange as it may seem.

After Mum, Dad and Bill returned to London and I was left alone in the cottage with John and Sylvia, my cousin Bill used to come and stay when his work allowed. I was nervous after the soldier incident, you see. Cousin Bill was in his early twenties and was exempt from national service because he had a health problem; instead, he worked on the railway. We grew very fond of each other. He could not come to stay very often but when he did we had quite a romantic time. He asked me to marry him but I was not prepared for that and I wouldn't have been able to anyway without my parents' consent. He played the piano well and I used to enjoy listening to him; he always used to finish the evening singing "Goodnight Sweetheart" to me. Mary and June Garfett came often to share our musical evenings. Mary took quite a shine to my cousin Bill — in fact, she came to the cottage one moonlit night when

42

I was on my own and threatened me in no uncertain terms to leave Bill alone. She came back the next day to apologise for her behaviour. She said she always behaved strangely at the time of the full moon. She had been employed as a nanny once but had to leave for this very reason. It was frightening.

Watching a country funeral was quite an experience, especially after seeing the showy affairs Londoners gave for their deceased relatives. I never enquired as to who made the coffin, but I know that the wreaths were made by the relatives, with flowers from the garden. The wire frames were removed from the grave a few days after the burial, then kept ready for the next funeral. An ordinary wagon from the farm was used to transport the coffin to its burial site and mourners would follow on foot. It was rather nice in some ways; but of course could never happen in the towns. Country living was a great experience for me. There were many strange sayings in Lincolnshire; the one I remember most was "Down yonder at the back end", which meant anything to do with the past.

After a while, when the air raids had quietened down in London, our parents decided we could move back. I packed everything for the removal van and got John, Sylvia and the two kittens ready for the journey, but the van didn't arrive until it was almost dark and in the end we had to clear the cottage by torchlight. We had spent all that day feeling bored and hungry and then we had to stay with Uncle Will and Aunt Dolly for the night. Our aunt wasn't pleased, especially about the kittens. The next day we set off for Muswell Hill in North

London. We could not return to our house in Hornchurch. It was still occupied by a soldier's wife and her children.

After we came back to London, Cousin Bill came down to see me a few times but we decided to call it a day. I had a different life yet again and took it in my stride. I bought a piece of sheet music, a romantic song and asked my mother to send it to my cousin, but I never got a reply. One day, many years later, when I was helping Mum sort out her bedroom I found the unsent letter. She just said, "Well, you couldn't marry a cousin anyway." I'd wondered why my letter was unanswered. I believe Cousin Bill died soon after the time I wrote the letter. I was never told properly, but I picked up hints from other members of the family. I have often wondered since, did our father ever write to us? I do realise Mother probably thought it was for the best; in those days parents did think they knew best and they behaved accordingly.

After about six months the soldier's wife in our house in Hornchurch did a moonlight flit, leaving our house in a poor condition. Dad went round each weekend to clean it before we could move back. By that time we had settled in Muswell Hill and I had got a job in the local cinema as an usherette. One week a particularly sad film was being shown three times a day. Each time it came on the screen I would be showing patrons to their seats sobbing my heart out. The manager had to transfer me to selling ice creams during the intervals so that I didn't see any of the film. I was amusing the patrons too much!

The next job I had was working in the City as a lift attendant. One day the manager of a firm called Canadian National Railways came out to ask me if I would like to work for them on their switchboard, which I did. I loved that job because it involved a lot of talking.

Then one day Mother heard on the radio that Fred's ship HMS *Vimera* had sunk soon after leaving Chatham naval base. In his last letter to his father he wrote, "I had to run all the way to the docks after my train was delayed. I very nearly did not make it. I did enjoy my leave." He would have been put on a charge had he not reported back in time. What a pity he ran so fast. Mother and I went to see Fred's father, Mr Mills, to see how he was coping with his double loss — his wife had died a few months previously.

Soon after this, Dad was able to move us all back to our original house in Hornchurch. We contacted Mr Mills and Mum invited him for Sunday dinner. He came often after that; Mother was very kind and always gave a helping hand to lame ducks, something I seem to have inherited.

Ted had also heard the sad news of the loss of his friend on the radio and when he next had leave he visited Mr Mills, who in turn brought Ted round to our house for Sunday dinner.

That's how our romance started. I did not like him in the old days, but he had grown up considerably and was far more mature. I think it was his blond hair I fell for at first; it was always golden. He too had lost his mother and his father had remarried and moved to

South Wigston, Leicestershire. He did not like spending his leave at home. Due to the dangerous work he was doing in the RAF, he received higher than average pay and he used to have 21 days' leave every three months, rather than the usual seven days. So we were able to get to know each other quite well. I would only be able to get a few days off from work but he used to meet me in London. Sometimes we would windowshop in Oxford Street and often saw a show, such as Ivor Novello's *Dancing Years*, or *King's Rhapsody*. We would also discuss our future. We always said we would have four children — two of each — but it did not work out like that. It turned out to be four boys. That suited us fine. I didn't really want girls anyway: I found housework and cooking so boring that I did not want to put a daughter through that. When number four came along I was so very pleased he was a boy. Ted was very proud of his sons.

Ted's leave came at Christmas one year and there was great excitement to have him home. He arrived a few days before Christmas Day so he helped with the preparations. In those days we used to save the cream from the milk to make butter. This was done by putting water in a jar, adding salt, then pouring the cream in. When the jar was three-quarters full, the lid was put on tightly and then whoever was willing would shake the jar vigorously until a ball of butter appeared. Well, this particular Christmas Eve Ted decided he would take on the chore of making the butter. So there he sat, shaking this jar. While he was doing it there was a knock at the door. It was a policeman to tell Ted he was to rejoin his unit at Aberporth, South Wales. He was to leave straight away, as a court of inquiry was being held to do with a plane crash two weeks earlier, and his presence was needed. Off he went in time to catch the last train back to Wales before Christmas. The journey took about 12 hours. When he reported to his unit he was told the inquiry was over and he wasn't needed at all! He could not get any rations while he was there and had to wait until the day after Boxing Day for a travel warrant to come back to Hornchurch. The same thing had happened to another airman and he and Ted spent a miserable Christmas Day walking around Aberporth and feeling very dejected. No rations and nothing to do; everywhere was closed. Then he had another 12-hour journey back. We did keep that butter for him, though. By the time he got back I had to go to work. He was just pleased to be home to food and a good sleep.

1944

I used to visit my Aunt Ivy each week on Tuesdays and stay overnight. It was 1944 and the doodlebug raids were starting. Aunt Ivy lived at the top of a three-storey house and we would lie in bed and watch the doodlebugs going across the sky. The doodlebugs were torpedo-like monstrosities which used to do a U-turn after their engines cut out and this was always the signal to run for shelter. We would leap out of bed and crawl underneath it, to wait for the bang. Once you heard it you knew you were safe — at least until the next one.

While visiting Ivy I caught scabies. Ivy used to visit a friend whose husband was posted in Italy, but had recently been home on leave. When Ivy got back from her first visit after that she started complaining about these itchy spots she had and asked me to put calamine lotion on them. A few days later I began to itch too, but I didn't have any spots and so didn't connect it with Ivy's. I went to a chemist and he suggested that I should buy some blood tonic. My parents were very amused when I came home with this huge bottle of Clark's Blood Tonic; there must have been about two pints of the wretched stuff. I took all the medicine in the bottle but still I itched. I decided to go to the doctor. We always tried to cure ourselves first, you see, but by then, enough was enough.

I'd noticed that the itching was worse at night, when I was warm in bed. When I looked at my arms I could see little faint red lines going from between my fingers up my arms. When I told the doctor, at first he said, "Just a bit of nerves bothering you."

I replied, "Are nerves catching, because my young sister has it now?"

"Actually," he said, "it's scabies you have. I was thinking it might be scabies, but knowing how clean your home is, I wasn't sure."

Then I told him of my visits to Auntie Ivy. He explained that the reason my itching had been worse at night was that the warmth of the bed made the little creatures more active and the faint red lines I had seen was where they were burrowing under my skin. The treatment he prescribed was rather harsh but it did clear the itch very quickly. Sylvia and I had to stand in front of a roaring fire with a fireguard round, scrub our skin with very hot water and a nailbrush to open the pores and then rub on the lotion. That lotion really stung and we had to put it everywhere, even our sensitive private areas. So it was not pleasant! Great entertainment, eh? Much better than today's TV!

Ted and I applied to our church in March 1944 for our wedding to take place in June during Ted's next leave. We were able to go and hear the banns read and the wedding was set for 11th June. Of course, D-Day was on 6th June, so it was only a few days after that. All leave was cancelled, but Ted's Commanding Officer let him come home as the banns had been read so long before. Ted's best friend was not allowed to come to be best man so Charles, a Czechoslovak friend of ours, stepped in to do the honours. He was an airman too, stationed at Hornchurch Aerodrome. Bill could not get leave to see me married. Ted's father came down from Leicestershire but the remainder of his family weren't able to come, due to the restrictions on entering our area. Friends from my office came though; I gave them a map showing them how to get there on foot so that the restrictions wouldn't matter. A number of people were caught and fined that day for entering Hornchurch; but, luckily, none of our friends were!

Of course we couldn't have the bells rung at the church but we did have six little choirboys; they cost me one shilling and sixpence each. I had to use my precious clothing coupons to buy the material for my wedding dress. It was ivory satin with sprays of lily of the valley on it and I still have it. A friend of mine made it for me, stitching every seam by hand. I needed a slip to wear under my dress so I had one made from parachute silk. This slip was also my nightdress. I wonder how many brides walk up the aisle ready for bed.

Sylvia and Kathleen, a neighbour's daughter, were my bridesmaids. Mother made her own dress and the bridesmaids' dresses all from material she got with our coupons. I knitted the bridesmaids' gloves and Mum's friend made her a hat. We made satin horseshoes and stitched sweet pea flowers to them for the bridesmaids to carry. A neighbour bought my bouquet — I was going to make one for myself with flowers out of the garden but she wouldn't hear of it. I was delighted with it when I saw it: pink carnations and gypsophila. Lennie, a friend of ours, gave us a 78 recording of "Ave Maria" as a present and we had that playing as we signed the register in the vestry.

We had a small reception that was held in Romford and then our guests walked back to our house for a party, maps at the ready. I managed to obtain a barrel of beer for the occasion — needless to say, the men enjoyed it. One of the neighbours had given my mother 72 pale pink peony blooms to decorate our house; it looked really lovely. After a few drinks from the barrel he gave us a rendition of "Red Sails in the Sunset" and "There'll Always Be An England" and we all joined in. It was such a pity Ted's sisters and Bill could not be there.

Our honeymoon, which was only one night, was spent in a neighbour's house, which Mrs Smale very kindly lent to us. Ted had to be back on duty the next day. I went back to work, leaving Mum to deal with the mess. Mums are wonderful people; we don't give them the thanks they deserve.

Soon after our marriage Ted was transferred to the Fleet Air Arm for training on aircraft carriers ready to go to the war zone in Japan. A lady on our road put it around that I was two-timing Ted when she saw me going around with a sailor. I did not enlighten her for a long time; she looked quite stupid when I did tell her that the sailor *was* Ted and he was now in the Navy.

I was still working in the City when the armistice was signed. I went with friends from the office to Buckingham Palace and stood at the railings. It was a wonderful feeling, calling "We want the King!" and singing patriotic songs. The King and Queen did come out on the balcony many times and the cheers were deafening. We had to walk back to Liverpool Street Station, but there were no trains and we couldn't get home. We had to sleep where we could. Mum and Dad were anxious; we never had phones in those days to let them know what we were doing. I'm glad we went to Buckingham Palace though; we couldn't have missed that great occasion. Similarly, very soon after VE Day, an impromptu concert was organised at the Royal Albert Hall. Representatives of all the forces that had taken part in the war paraded in, including all of the free forces from other countries and the voluntary organisations, like the Home Guard. The King and Queen were there. We had seats up in the "gods". The atmosphere was electric — all that cheering, singing and clapping. I am so pleased I went; I'll never forget it. We walked all through Hyde Park afterwards singing songs like "It's a Long Way to Tipperary", "Show Me the Way to Go Home", "Nelly Dean", and, course, "Knees Up, Mother Brown" — we were singing all the way to Liverpool Street. Once again we'd missed the last train. We were so happy that we didn't mind; Mum did, though, because I hadn't been able to tell her where I was. Obviously she was worried. It must have been awful for mothers at home, worrying about their offspring going out — especially with the war on. We youngsters took it all in our stride. Now I realise just what mothers go through and how selfish we were then.

Soon after this I was given notice to leave my job, because it was not the policy of the company to employ married women in peacetime. They suggested to me that I should write to Barclays Bank for a job. I laughed and said, "They would never employ me," but they said I should try and suggested that I ask to work for a small branch rather than Head Office. Much to my astonishment they did offer me a job and I went to Spitalfields Branch. I was told to make myself useful until a vacancy came up at the bank school, so I could be taught how to do the work.

Have you ever heard of brain ache? I certainly had it for a couple of weeks. I had to concentrate all the time, which I found hard after my comparatively easy job. You see, I had to go straight in and do the work there and then. There was no room for passengers; so many of the staff were still in the forces. I had not a clue how to set up the Remington Rand machine or back the worksheet with carbon paper. I had to do what I suppose is called spreadsheets today. All the figures for the cheques and money that came over the counter had to be put in various columns and at the end of the day everything had to cross balance — if it didn't, we had to stay until the mistakes were found. They were usually found quickly, but I always dreaded that the error would be mine, especially if it was on a Saturday morning when everyone was keen to be off for the weekend. By the time a vacancy came up at the bank school the manager said there was no point in my going. He said, "You know more now than they would ever teach you."

At lunchtime we used to run to Bishopsgate and catch a bus to Head Office in Gracechurch Street to go to the Barclays Bank luncheon club. We would get very good food, waitress service, silver cutlery and white starched tablecloths. Also I would enjoy a glass of port wine — my favourite tipple. It was all at a very low cost and was absolute luxury considering we were still on rations. Of course, we had the rush back to the bank afterwards, but it was worth it.

On Fridays I usually went with the bank messenger to Head Office, carrying a leather holdall full of cash, which would be strapped to our wrists. A taxi would always be waiting to take us. When we got there we would go down to the vaults where we had to pass through a turnstile with a guard on duty. Each branch had its own cell down there, so that the money was kept separate from the money of all the other branches. The guard would unlock ours, the straps on our wrists were removed and the messenger would place the cash on the floor and pick up whatever he was required to take back. We would then go to cages on the top floor to collect the cheques for our branch that had been cleared by the clearing-house.

While I was working in Spitalfields I realised I was pregnant. I told the manager and he was quite happy for me to continue working there. I was working quite close to Petticoat Lane, where the market is and one day during my lunch hour I managed to buy a baby's white enamel bath, about 36 inches long and 18 wide. I was so happy because baby equipment was almost impossible to get. I must have amused or annoyed everybody by taking this huge bath back to the bank, but they were too polite to comment. I also must have looked a pretty sight travelling home on the train with this bath and very pregnant as well.

The war ended quite suddenly due to that terrible bomb dropped on Japan. Ted was demobbed a few months later and Mum and Dad said we could live with them until we got our own home. Ted duly went to get his demob clothes — a light navy suit with a wide chalk stripe. It fitted where it touched but even so it was better than nothing; his old civvies didn't fit either.

Ted was able to go back to his old job as a joiner, but after a while he instead went to work on the now obsolete troop ships, to turn them back to their former glory — before the war they were luxury liners, you see.

Quite a lot of pilfering went on in the docks. Men made a lot of furniture and had it hidden on lorries so they could take it home. The only thing Ted ever pinched was a piece of plywood to make a bed table for me to have my meals off when the baby was born. We used to stay in bed for a week after the birth in those days. He shoved this bit of plywood up his jumper and walked out of the docks and all was well until he went to sit down on the train. The wood gave him a mighty bash under his chin and the other passengers all roared out laughing.

I was able to stay at the bank until early November and our baby was due in December. It was arranged that I would return to work after the birth, but I decided not to go back; when he was born I did not want to leave him. Anyway, it would have been too much for Mum to look after him as well as the rest of the family. Both my doctor and nurse had said while I was pregnant that the baby was tiny and was probably a girl, because of the strong heartbeat. I had my confinement at home and when our baby did not arrive near the expected date, my midwife suggested I take a four-ounce bottle of castor oil and have a very hot mustard bath. I don't recommend consuming castor oil; it is the most obnoxious thing I have ever swallowed. After the bath and the castor oil I spent the whole night looking like a red turkey cock and trying desperately hard not to burp. I had a few twinges that night but I took no notice of them. And our baby was not born until two weeks later! So much for castor oil!

When our baby did decide to come, his arrival was quite hasty. I think he remembered that castor oil and thought, "I am not having any more of that jollop. I am moving out as soon as possible."

Just before the labour started on 23rd December, 1946, Ted had popped out to the local pub, because we had heard that they'd had a delivery of beer. There was a queue of people all hoping to get some for Christmas. He came back grinning like a Cheshire Cat with a couple of bottles and was immediately dispatched to go and fetch the midwife as things had been happening in his absence! My midwife arrived and said, "We should have baby here by morning." The family were gathered in the dining room and were all amazed at our baby's fast arrival, one hour before midnight. After what the doctor had said about the baby being a girl I had visions of a tiny blonde girl looking like her dad, but instead he was a nine-pound boy with a mop of black hair! We named him Christopher. The doctor was amazed; he had thought I had a very little baby. Needless to say Ted's purchase at the pub was soon consumed; even the doctor had a drink.

January 1947 was the worst weather for years and coal was rationed. Due to my having a newborn baby I was allowed priority coal ration so we were some of the fortunate few and all sat round the only fire in the house. Sylvia had passed the scholarship and John was studying for the eleven-plus; they also joined us in the only warm room to do their homework. I often think it must have been hard for them with a young baby in the house. Christopher became spoilt because I used to feed him at all hours, including whenever he awoke in the night. Often he was still there in the morning slurping away happily. Anything rather than wake the whole household with his yelling. Consequently, he needed attention at night for many years.

My first outing after the birth was to go and arrange the christening and be "churched". This is not a custom carried out these days, but back then, should you not have been churched you would not have been welcomed in any of your friends' homes. They were quite strict on that point.

I used to bath Christopher each morning before his ten o'clock feed. Then I would wrap him up warm in his pram and push him up the garden, bumpity-bump, over the ice and snow, until his two o'clock feed was due. It was a ritual I believed was the correct thing to do, even when it was raining. Only when it was foggy was he not taken out. Our bedrooms were so very cold, so I suppose he did not notice the weather much. Water pipes in our house were often frozen and oil lamps had to be put upstairs to stop the loo from freezing up. The cold weather lasted until March.

I took to wearing Ted's bell-bottomed trousers to keep me warm — they were great. Luckily we had a glorious summer to follow the awful winter.

One day Christopher was up the garden in his pram and we had decorators busy repairing the war damage to Mum's house, when all of a sudden a whirlwind blew! The sky turned black as night. I rushed up the garden and grabbed Christopher from his pram and by the time I reached the house the pram had blown over. The decorators came down from their ladders in record time and it was all over in a few minutes. The dust and filth that was blown around was unbelievable in such a short space of time. It was quite frightening.

1948 — The Next Chapter in Our Lives

We finally moved into our own home in July 1948. Mum was upset as she missed us all. We had a very nice council house, on the edge of the new estate, but we had only very basic furniture at that time, all secondhand.

My second son, John, was born in 1952 and was a fine, bonny nine-pounder. Ted had arranged to have his week's holiday for the week our baby was expected, but of course baby once again was in no hurry to come into the world, so Ted was back at work by the time of the birth. Fortunately, John arrived in the early hours of the morning, so Ted was at home for it, although the midwife would not let him into the room until about five minutes after the birth.

An awful practice they had in those days was to circumcise male babies and the midwife and doctor came round to circumcise John when he was only two weeks old. I was told to prepare the dining table with a clean sheet and a pillow and to put the radio on loud and run the water so I wouldn't be able to hear anything. But of course I did hear him cry. He was then handed back to me, poor little mite, sobbing. "He will soon forget when he has had his feed," the doctor said. My neighbour usually changed his nappies for me, or Ted would if he was around. I was given a small bottle of Friar's Balsam which I had to pour on the wound should it bleed, but fortunately, it did not. I had to go through all this again with Gerald after he was born in 1956. It was barbaric.

The time spent in Lincolnshire stood me in good stead for managing. I knew how to sweep floors by dampening them before brushing to keep the dust down and I knew about washing the clothes on a rubbing board and mangling them. Clothes lines were strung across the living room during the night in winter, as often when I brought the clothes in from the garden they would be frozen stiff and the shirts and trousers would stand like little boys until they defrosted. Ted and I would often have toast and cocoa sitting between dangling wet sheets with a fire roaring in the hearth. We were usually very tired but happy. All the washing was removed before the children came down to breakfast. They would have enjoyed playing hide-and-seek amongst the lines of washing, but I could not stand that early in the morning.

Christopher was six years old before we could afford a vacuum cleaner. I had my first washing machine when my third child, Gerald, was seven years old. This came about because Mum wanted me to have a demonstration of the new Hoover Twin Tub washing machine in my kitchen; I don't know why she didn't have it in her own house. I was so impressed and thrilled with the machine's capabilities that I said to the demonstrator I'd buy it there and then. An insurance policy we owned had just matured so I had the money for it. After the man had gone I realised I hadn't discussed it with Ted. He was away working at the time, so that evening I sat down and tried to compose a letter to him explaining what I'd done. Suddenly I heard activity in the hall and when I went to look there was Ted; he'd come home earlier than expected. I just stood there going, "Ooh aah oooh," and he said, "What have you done?" But after giving him a demonstration of this weird and wonderful machine and singing its praises, all was forgiven: Ted agreed that buying it had been a good idea.

Ted worked very hard at this time. When the dockworkers came out on strike he and his friend left immediately. They went to work shop-fitting for the Co-op. He could not afford to be off work and usually worked overtime on Saturdays and Sundays, but always tried to be home to read to the children before they went to bed. One morning he got up as usual and went off to the station only to find it closed — it was Good Friday, a national holiday. He was so used to getting up and going out early that he just did it automatically. We were all still asleep when he got back and were very surprised when he came up with a cup of tea. We all had a good laugh over that.

After a while he was sent to work in Wales which meant he was away three months at a time. He used to parcel up his dirty washing and send it to me. I would send his clean clothes back; no launderettes in those days, you see. Then he was sent to Oxford and that was not so bad; he could afford to come home every six weeks. When my third child Gerald was born in 1956 Ted was allowed to work from the local depot for about a year. He always cycled to work and it was about 13 miles each way.

Soon after Christopher started school he got tonsillitis about every three weeks. The paediatrician decided he should have his tonsils removed and eventually the day came for him to have his operation. Before taking him to the hospital I went to see my neighbour, Betty, knowing that the birth of her fourth child was due. Her doctor told her she had started her labour that morning, so when I arrived home from the hospital I cooked Ted and John's meal, put John to bed and said, "I will just pop in to see Betty and her baby." I reached her house only to find her sitting by the fire looking very uncomfortable, still with no baby. I suggested to her husband that he should go and see the midwife, Nurse Willis, to tell her she would probably be needed fairly soon. Then I suggested to Betty that we should light a fire in the next room, where she was going to have the baby. There I was, trying to draw the fire up with newspaper when Betty had a severe pain. I went over and rubbed her back and then had returned to the fire with more papers when I heard the pop of her waters breaking. I tried to mop it up, took her soiled clothing off and ran to the kitchen sink with it, retching all the way. When I went back into the room Betty was having another severe pain. Next thing, the baby was born and at that moment her husband was knocking on the front door. I shouted to him, "Go and get Nurse Willis," but luckily she was already on her way over. Betty's husband did a disappearing trick; we did not see him until the early hours of the morning.

All this hassle had its good side. It saved me from worrying about Christopher all that night. We were not allowed to visit him for another week.

Eighteen months later Betty was expecting another baby. Les, her husband, put a note through my letterbox on his way to work, asking me to send Christopher for Nurse Willis. Betty had started her labour. I gave my children their breakfasts and had them ready for school — except for Gerald who was still in his pram. So we all trooped round to Betty's to see how she was getting on. Her children hadn't had their breakfast, nor were they ready for school, so I got them sorted and sent them all off together. I put Ian, Betty's youngest, in his pram alongside Gerald in the hall. In came Nurse Willis. I was quite nervous of her; she was very tall and had a loud voice. "This baby cannot be born in here!" she boomed. You see, there were no net curtains and Betty's bed was by the window. I could only think of getting my curtains from my window — I knew they would fit. So that was what I did. Baby Sheila was born about lunchtime and then home came five hungry children for their dinners. I managed to find some food for them. While all this activity was going on my mother was patiently waiting for me; I had promised to meet her to go Christmas shopping. She was furious when I didn't turn up.

A neighbour who lived opposite me said she thought the whole affair was disgusting — apparently she could see just what was going on, through those curtains. I replied if all she had to do all day was stand and watch she should feel ashamed: a little help would have been better. Needless to say, she never spoke to me again. Then to top it all, Betty's husband complained to me that he hadn't found out his daughter had been born until his foreman told him at about four o'clock that afternoon. I had traipsed a long way with all the children with me to find a call box, so you can imagine what I said to him. No, it is unprintable.

John was a very mischievous child; he used to squeeze himself in at the back of the gas cooker to try and reach the flame that he could see flickering there. We had a very small kitchen so the children usually had to sit in the pram while I did the cooking or ironing. Washing I did while they were in bed for the night. I used to give them all kinds of things to play with. I had a playpen for John — he would drag it across the room, so to keep it still I used to fix it to a big armchair. Then that too would find its way across the room! In the garden he would manage to move the pen across the lawn until he was near the flowerbeds and could play with the dirt through the bars. He was also very much a home boy. When he got a bit older he always bought a plant for the garden out of his pocket money each week. One year he saved a little every week at the local sweet shop to buy an Easter egg for me. It was a big one with a design of a hot air balloon to commemorate the release of the film *Around the World in Eighty Days*. When the shopkeeper asked him, "Is it for you?" John replied, "No, it's for my mum."

One day my neighbour and friend, Winnie, suggested we take our broods out for the day — she being the proud mother of five children and myself the proud mother of three, there were a lot of us! We finally decided on a trip to the London Zoo. We had a very good day. I eagerly pointed out where I used to live, the church and school I had attended — which could all be seen from the zoo. At the end of the day we decided to have a trip to Paddington on a long boat along the Regent's Canal. Luckily the children were all extremely well-behaved as they were so tired by then — I was worried that if they were naughty we wouldn't be allowed on. We were all waiting in the queue for the boat and as it got nearer our turn the porter put out his arm and said, "Sorry ladies, this boat is full. It's the last boat today." However, he took one look at all our disappointed faces and suggested we could sit on the top of the canal boat. That was a comedy in itself, getting us all up on top — the children were OK, they got up in a flash, but I've never been very agile. Chris had to give me a bunk-up. Winnie was a lady of large proportions and also had problems. And then we had to get the pushchair up! The crew and the other passengers found it very amusing. We had to remove our shoes in case they fell off as we had our legs dangling over the side. Going under the bridges had us worried at first, but there turned out to be plenty of headroom. The kids yelled and giggled whenever we came to a bridge. The hardest part was when we had to get off, what with pins and needles in our feet and having to sort out all the children's shoes and put them back on. Then we had to find our way to Paddington Station. We arrived home very, very tired and grubby but happy.

There was always a panic of some sort going on where we lived; one early morning Betty came running round to our kitchen door saying that Stewart, her eldest son, had cut off the tops of his fingers with a razor blade his father had left lying around. Christopher just folded the fingertips back and wrapped them up. I couldn't look and ran upstairs, along with one of Chris's friends who happened to be there at the time. How Chris kept so calm I'll never know. Not many weeks after this, one day I heard Betty screaming at my door. Stewart had climbed up on a table and unravelled some electric wiring that had not been made safe. The wires were stuck in his hand between the thumb and forefinger. I went in and turned off the electricity. Very fortunately for Stewart, he happened to be wearing plimsolls; otherwise, I don't think he would have survived. On neither of these occasions was he seen by a doctor, although that electric burn took months to heal. Les, his father, would have been in deep trouble if the doctor had been called.

Like the older boys, Gerald was fond of music at an early age. By the time he was two years old he would stand at the record player picking out records he liked — they were never vocal pieces and his favourite was "Flight of the Bumblebee". He was also always very good at taking things to pieces — including his cot. We always knew when he woke up because shortly afterwards we would hear the side of his cot hitting the floor. As he grew older he would join every organisation that came to the district. He joined the Romford Drum and Trumpet Corps. He had to learn how to march before he first saw an instrument, though, so he didn't last long at that. Then he came home with an old police uniform for me to alter for him. He wanted to be in the St John's Ambulance Brigade, which was impossible, of course. Then he joined the Cubs and the chess club and then the Vikings when he was much older.

We were also the proud owners of various pets: budgies, goldfish, cats that were usually pregnant, tortoises and guinea pigs. The guinea pigs used to come and stand by me and make a chirping noise when I was pegging out the washing. I got quite fond of them. I'd like to mention it was usually me who had to look after all those animals — the novelty soon wore off for the children.

Gerald and John used to meet their dad off the train on Saturdays; he always had a bag full of various sweets for them and a bunch of flowers for me. One day a policeman was also waiting at the station and Gerald said to him, "Could I see your truncheon? I want to be a policeman when I grow up." John was so embarrassed. He never went to the station again to meet Ted.

Ted did try to cultivate our garden, being a craftsman. But he was a perfectionist too and wanted the lawns and flowerbeds to be always immaculate and that was an impossible task. What with working overtime most weekends, by the time he was able to have another session in the garden weeds would have appeared everywhere. Also there would be big holes and trenches where the boys had been playing goodies and baddies. A neighbour's little girl came in one day to play. She really enjoyed herself and when she got home, she said to her mother, "The Ellards have a lovely garden." Her mother was feeling quite envious until the girl continued, "It's all big trenches and very hilly, I've had a wonderful time." Ted wasn't sure if or how he was to take that as a compliment and, needless to say, he gave up the idea of a perfect garden. In the end he was pleased that the children enjoyed the shambles. I expect you are wondering why I didn't keep them in order in the garden! Well, secretly I liked them all out there, so that I could see what they were up to.

John learnt the guitar. He enjoyed playing the instrument, but doing the written homework was usually left to me, just before he had to go to his lesson! Chris was crazy about classical music and also Jazz and Rock 'n' Roll: Louis Armstrong, Django Reinhardt, Buddy Holly, Fats Domino, Dizzy Gillespie. He bought a trumpet and drove all his classmates mad; his only topic of conversation was music. One day when the post came Chris had 27 letters from various regiments inviting him to go for interviews to join their bands. I was shocked and said, "I never knew you wanted to join the army." He replied, "I don't." Then we realised his friends at school had done this as a prank. He never told them about the letters until much later; he kept them wondering. However, he did go for an interview

— it was a tank regiment in Dorset. The music master there advised him to stay on at school and get his A-levels; he (the music master) would then see that he went to Kneller Hall, the army music training college. He did all this and eventually joined the 3rd Carabineers: The Prince of Wales Dragoon Guards.

During this time I was working four days a fortnight at the London Stock Exchange, on account days to collate share certificates, ready for posting. We had to complete all the work that came through each day and there was so much to be done in such a short space of time that often we had to work on the Saturday too.

In 1965 Sir Winston Churchill died and I went with my mother and younger brother John to Ludgate Hill to pay homage to our great leader. His speeches and confidence had helped to keep our spirits up all through that dreadful war. We stood all night to pay our respects and see his coffin pulled through the streets of London, with his various medals and honours displayed on it. It was something we felt we had to do for such a great man. Lord Mountbatten and other dignitaries all walked behind the coffin and royalty and heads of state from all over the world followed in coaches. I remember seeing General de Gaulle and also King Peter of Yugoslavia — he was gorgeous, I really fell for him. I have since visited Churchill's home at Westerham — such a lovely family home — and seen his paintings. And, of course, his goldfish, which he used to feed every day.

While I was working at the Stock Exchange I found out I was pregnant. I was nervous about having to tell my eldest son this news, but his reaction was, "Good for you, Mum." He and his friends used to call in at all times of the day for coffee. They were studying for their A-levels and had lots of free periods. My delicate state did not bother them one bit.

Chris still did not tell the boys at school he was going into the army until just before he left. They were most surprised when he announced it, especially as he never said a word about the prank they had played upon him. The school staff and headmaster were amazed too, because Chris hated any form of exercise and was always late for school. While he was still a raw recruit he was interviewed one morning by Jack de Manio on the radio after the early morning news and asked why he had turned down a university place to join the army. He said it was his love of music. He was told later that he was the brainiest musician in the British Army at that time.

Naturally I was upset when he went off to the army but I still had two lads at home to keep me busy. I was also getting ready for the new baby. Ted was still working long hours.

John had a difficult time at school; he was off school for a few months after contracting pneumonia at the age of six and missed a lot of basic work. When he returned to school the headmaster insisted on his being placed in the top group, saying he was an A-stream child. John did not find catching up with the others easy. When they sat exams he came out at the bottom of the class and it ruined his confidence. I went to the school many times asking for his group to be changed and eventually he was put in a lower stream and his confidence improved. It was too late to pass the eleven-plus by then, but he has done well for himself with an HND in engineering.

I continued to work at the Stock Exchange until I was four months into my pregnancy. The day I left, I and six of my colleagues went to The Frog, which was what we called the pub in Throgmorton Avenue. Women were not welcome in there. As we strode in, one man said, "Is somebody getting married?" I said, "Me." The expressions on their faces had to be seen to be believed.

How things have changed these last few years; at that time how busy I was, with two boys and a new baby on the way. Robert was born on 19th December, 1965, almost 19 years after the birth of our first baby, Christopher. All of our children were born at home, so although Ted was not allowed to be with me during my labour, he was always there to hold the babies as soon as they were born.

Chris had joined the band by then and was stationed in Detmold in Germany. I. O. Herbert, the master of the Regimental Band, had fulfilled his promise and got Chris a place at Kneller Hall. He learnt to play the trumpet and the cornet.

While in Germany he met a very nice German girl called Anneleise. Her first introduction to the Ellard family came in February 1966. She had a stormy crossing over the English Channel and we welcomed her into our home, but what a reception she had! It was unfortunate that at that time our youngest son, Robert, who was three months old, had a tummy bug. We had brought his cot down to the living room and there were wet sheets and countless other items of laundry strung across the kitchen to dry, so it was quite chaotic. Anneleise came in and immediately picked Robert up and cuddled him. She took to us and we to her; that is how it has always stayed. Christopher and Anneleise married in July 1967 in Germany. We could not attend the wedding due to various commitments, but they did have a blessing in our local church in Tonbridge in 1968.

1967

We felt that as Ted was getting older he should look for another job which did not involve too much travelling. It took him a couple of years to find somewhere, but eventually he accepted a position as manager at Marslands of Edenbridge, a new double-glazing firm. He had one month's holiday a year plus sick pay, which was something we had never experienced. Ted always used to have to buy stamps each week from his wages to cover his one week's leave, Christmas, Bank Holidays and any times when he was off sick. He also now didn't have to leave the house until half past eight in the morning and only had half an hour's journey, which was through the lovely Kentish countryside. It was quite a bonus! Once the new job was settled we had to find somewhere to live. We were offered a place at Edenbridge by the LCC, but the rooms of the house were so small that we wouldn't have been able to get all the family and the furniture in.

After studying maps, we decided to try and buy something in Tonbridge. This too became another complete change to our lives, after living in a London suburb. We found a house in Tonbridge, a small country market town was then, and when we were finally settled I would take the family down to the Farmers' market day on a Tuesday to watch the cattle being auctioned and then loaded on to vans to be taken to their new farms. Quite a novelty to us, also. About 50 yards up the road from where we lived I would take Robert to watch the cows grazing on Mabledon farm. That too was a strange experience. Also we could go to Lambsie Bank and look down on cattle grazing and the oast house. My German daughter-in-law and her mother really loved our walks over there. A new motorway has been constructed through this area, making it easier for traffic to go Tunbridge Wells. I do admit it was needed, so the geography of that area quickly changed.

My brother and sister were extremely good; for one thing, they helped us financially for the first month before Ted was paid. Then, later, they helped us with the deposit for the house we had found. I am telling you all this to explain why I took a job doing night work at the hospital in Hornchurch. Gerald had passed the eleven-plus so there was his uniform to be bought as well as all the expenses for the removal. John and Gerald were so good, looking after Robert while I was working — before we moved, Ted was having to leave home at half past five every morning in order to get to work in Edenbridge by nine o'clock. They always got my breakfast ready for when I came home in the morning; usually it was a boiled egg. The only thing they wouldn't do was change Robert's nappy, which was understandable. The nappy was always dangling around Robert's feet by the time I got home.

During that summer I developed gall bladder problems that developed into pancreatitis. I spent the best part of the autumn in hospital. Fortunately, we had found a new, four-bedroom house in Tonbridge before I was taken ill. My brother John had helped us with this too, taking us down to look at properties every weekend. All the negotiations were going through when I became ill. Mother came and collected Robert, plus his cot, pram, highchair and clothes. He was 18 months old — that difficult stage. He was hard work for Mum and Dad. Mum and brother John used to take him down to Southend beach each evening so he could run around, to tire him out!

Ted used to break his journey home each evening to come and visit me in the hospital. He only just made it; visiting was only allowed from seven o'clock until half past and the ward sister was very strict. Sometimes his visits only lasted five minutes. So, all in all, it was a hard year. Once again, Sylvia was very good and made all the removal arrangements and our son John also helped all he could. He was just getting on well with his education at that time. It was such a pity to have to move him, but when you have children there is never a right time to move, one that will suit all the family. I was not allowed out of hospital to help with the move.

One strange thing we later discovered was that Bill and his wife had just bought their first house, moved the same day as us and paid the same price for it as we had for ours! They were living in Scotland then. In fact, quite a few coincidences have occurred throughout our lives. That's twins for you! We hadn't especially kept in touch, so this business with the houses came as a complete surprise to us.

We moved in November 1967. The week following the move Christopher came home for the weekend from Kneller Hall. During his return journey the train he was travelling on was involved in a crash at Hither Green. When he was able, he telephoned the hospital to let me know he was safe and Matron let me go in her room to speak to him. He kept saying, "Why me?" You see, he was not hurt although others around him had been killed. A baby he had wrapped in his jacket had died. Chris was ill later and had to go straight to the sick bay when he arrived back at Kneller Hall. He said that the people who lived in the houses around the crash site were very good to him. I regret that I did not get in touch with them later, to thank them.

I was allowed home for Christmas. I cooked all the usual Christmas goodies but I was on a very strict diet — only a very little turkey breast, Brussels sprouts, one potato and the inevitable jelly. I had jelly every day for my dinner in hospital, a diabetic one. So my Christmas dinner was a real banquet, but I enjoyed cooking for the others.

1968

I went back to Oldchurch Hospital in Romford for the operation in January 1968; they looked after me so well. I felt confident with them, so I was pleased I was allowed to have the operation there. The NHS looked after me very well. Visitors were few — my family could not visit because of the distance, Mother was busy with Robert. Occasionally an ex-neighbour came and once Chris came. He had travelled from Twickenham and the weather was very cold, icy and snowy. It was about nine o'clock in the evening but the staff nurse let him in and he stayed with me for about half an hour. He must have had a long journey back to Kneller Hall! I was thrilled to see him. I knew I was on the road to recovery by then. I always said I would never grumble or complain again, but of course I do.

We became well known in Tonbridge due to Anneleise — my new daughter-in-law — coming to live with us. I was known as "that rich woman with the German *au pair*"!

I found a part-time job for Anneleise and myself at the local zip factory. Anneleise was very amused; she had never been in a factory before. We worked from six o'clock in the evening until nine o'clock, measuring zips. We used to have a very enjoyable time; it was more like a social evening than a proper job, much to the forelady's annoyance. Getting that job was the best thing I could have done. I got to know a large number of people from Tonbridge through working there, so they no longer called me "that rich woman with the *au pair*". I also became friends with Josie, another employee at the factory and we are still great friends. Her knowledge of Tonbridge and local gossip was very helpful to me at the time.

Anneleise and Chris had married in a registry office in Germany and now wanted to have their marriage blessed before the birth of their first baby in June. So it was arranged for the day of Anneleise's 21st birthday, in February. Her mother came over from Germany and all of our family came from Essex. Chris looked very smart in his dress uniform and I made Anneleise a dress that did not show her bump too much. We had a reception at home afterwards.

The following June our first grandchild, Steven, was born. Robert ran around telling everyone, "I am Uncle Bob!" Steven was christened in September, at the time of the awful floods in Tonbridge. The flooding didn't affect us as we lived high on Quarry Hill and we were so busy with preparations for the christening party that we hadn't heard the news. We were most surprised when our guests did not turn up for the christening. No one was even able to contact us to explain, as all the phone lines were out of order. We only found out when we arrived at the church later in the day. We had

Anneleise's mother and brother staying with us and they had to stay an extra week due to the transport difficulties.

After a while Chris's regiment was stationed in Chester, so he and his family had to move up there. Anneleise missed Ted; he was the only person who could get Steven to sleep.

John was not happy at his new school; he found the standard of education lower than it had been at Hornchurch. Gerald did not settle well at his school either. At the end of his third year we had to attend the open evening for parents to discuss their child's progress. Ted and I went early, hoping to miss some of the staff, as we had a feeling all was not well. We were met at the entrance by Mr Davies, the headmaster, and Ted introduced us as Gerald's parents.

"Ah, yes," he said, "Gerald Ellard!!"

He asked us what Gerald did in his spare time. "Not a lot," says I, "he's usually in his room doing his homework and listening to music."

"That's what you think," came the reply. "Your son is the secretary for the Schools' Action Union, which sends out leaflets asking students to support the idea of pupils having some say in the running of their school, including questions regarding discipline and school uniforms. They also want to meet the school governors to put across their ideas." This was revolutionary in those days, when we were still living in an era of children being seen and not heard; now it is common practice.

John met Yvonne, a very pleasant girl from Sevenoaks and they married in 1973. John had just finished his apprenticeship with Wallace and Tiernan, an engineering firm in Tonbridge, while Yvonne travelled to London each day to work at the Home Office as a secretary. John eventually found employment in Crawley, where they are now living. Their first son, David, was born while Ted and I were in Washington. Then along came Mark, their second son; he has always been interested in electrics. As a toddler he was quite happy walking around with a toaster under his arm. He thought it was much better than a teddy!

Ted felt it was time he learnt to drive, so we bought a car and he passed his test first time. We decided to go on holiday to Greatstone and we took my mother, Gerald and Bob. As we were approaching the house we were going to rent, I said, "There it is!" Ted replied, "It can't be, there are people in the garden." At that moment, while we were all peering at the house, our car caught the side of a pile of asphalt, which was covered by grass. We rebounded off it into the car that was parked outside the house we were renting. It was a brand new Rover and the owners were not pleased. After much grovelling we were allowed to enter the house. After that I had to climb over the brake to the driver's side in order to get out; my side was jammed. Another time we went to Dungeness and parked on the stony beach where a number of other cars were parked, only to discover we were unable to drive away. The more Ted tried, the deeper we seemed to sink.

Fortunately, a lorry full of workmen happened to be passing and they stopped and hauled us off the beach. By then we were fully initiated into the joys of driving!

The zip factory closed down and I needed to get another job. We were paying John and Sylvia the money we owed them by standing order, so we had to keep the bank balance steady. I eventually found another job in Langton Green; my employer was Kashfi Shah, wife of Idries Shah, a philosopher, writer, etc. It was supposed to have been only for six weeks but in fact I stayed seven years. I was able to take Bob with me as there was a nanny, Kay, who looked after my employer's children.

Bob settled in well. We used to catch the bus each morning at eight o'clock; the journey took an hour. I started the job in February and the snow was very deep when we got off the bus each morning. Bob loved walking across the Green with ours the only footprints on the newly-fallen snow and he enjoyed the lovely crunch the crisp snow made beneath our feet. I only worked mornings at first. My employer was a philosopher and author who worked mainly at home. He had three children. There was Saira, who was four years old, and twins called Tahir and Safia who were both one year old. Bob was three years old then, so he fitted in quite well. Kay was needed to keep the children well occupied and I kept a watchful eye on Bob.

Gradually I began to work full time. A nursery class was opened and a few children from outside came. They had school dinners and I was in charge of making the sweet each day. The house had an Aga and I enjoyed the delights of cooking with it. In the fullness of time I did quite a lot of cooking there: Simnel cakes, Christmas cakes, Christmas puddings, birthday cakes. I even used to give the children cookery lessons.

I met many interesting people while working there. Robert Graves used to enjoy my Cornish pasties and Robert Dougal liked my apple pies — he came and gave a lecture on his work with the BBC. I was also interested to meet General Glubb Pasha, Sir Mortimer Wheeler, and several authors and actors.

There was also a film made there for the BBC as part of the *One Pair of Eyes* series. There was a garden party, with a lamb roast cooked on a spit. I was asked questions during the filming. I tried to think sensibly but my mind literally went blank. I do appear in the film, but only for about half a minute. A champagne party was held at the end of filming. Ted didn't come, preferring to stay at home and tinker with the car, but Bob enjoyed himself; he was showered with champagne when the corks were being popped.

On our journeys home from work Bob was always keen for me to learn what he had been taught that day. He would write Arabic letters on the steamed-up windows of the bus and would want me to recite Arabic words. He always called me Mrs Ellard like the other children and staff at Langton House. The funniest thing was when he wanted me to sing. I have always had difficulty keeping in tune. Much to the amusement of the other passengers, Bob used to say, "Lift your voice,

Mrs Ellard!" It was so funny. How I wish those days were back again.

There was a Swiss lad who came to Langton House as an *au pair* and to learn English. He was nicknamed J. He temporarily acted as the Nanny to help look after the children when Kay became ill. He was great fun, either hindering or helping me with my chores. One day he came to help me polish the Durbar Room. There had been a big reception so the floor needed some attention. It certainly had that; he sploshed the polish all over the floor then proceeded to teach me to do the jitterbug, until we heard a voice calling, "J, where are you? The donkey needs feeding." I was furious because I then had to get down on all fours and use elbow grease to get the floor back to its former glory.

Eventually Pauline came to take up the post of nanny and she too brightened up life considerably — she has a great sense of humour. The children loved her and I am still very friendly with her.

Jack, my stepfather, died in 1975 and then in the spring of 1976 I lost my mother. I had often gone to stay with her at weekends because her health was failing. Upon reflection I now realise that I treated Bob as I had been treated — I didn't explain to him the reason why I left him with Ted each weekend and when Mum died I didn't explain that to him either. Of course he knew, but I completely forgot his feelings. He was only eleven and very fond of her.

It was at about this time that we learnt with great sadness that Chris was leaving Anneleise. They had always seemed so well-suited and young Steven was devoted to his parents. We had many happy holidays with them and Amelia, Anneleise's mother. Eventually Christopher met and married Erica. She came from the Black Forest region of Germany and so he has now set up home there. They have a son called Sebastian. Ted and I have spent happy times with them and Erica's family and friends have always given us a great welcome. Ted had a quirky sense of humour and Chris's friends liked him very much; he always used to try and speak German with them and the laughter used to ring out. As for me, I can only remember *ja bitte* and *nein danke*!

My twin died in January 1987 and I miss him very much. I went to Scotland to see him in December 1986 and we spent a lot of time chatting, which is when he spoke of the various things that I have written about. When he had his last heart attack, on his way to the hospital, he said to his wife, "Now, don't go phoning Peggy and worrying her." Those were the last words he spoke.

When Pauline, who had been the nanny at Langton House, was due to give birth to her second child, I jokingly said, "I'll deliver it for you." Little did I know I would be greatly involved and I often think of the saying, "There's many a true word spoken in jest". Her husband did not feel he wanted to attend the birth, so she asked me to be there. One evening she rang to say the time had come. Ted drove me to her house and took us to hospital. I stayed with her and was the first person to cuddle young Lawrence. I won't go into details but I can say I know more about her person than she does herself!

As Bob grew older Ted and I thought he should go to the ordinary school, as it would not have been fair to him to stay in the nursery class any longer. I am sure it was hard for him at first. He was a borderline candidate for grammar school and as we had already had experiences of John's struggles to keep up, it was decided he should go to the local senior school instead. This did turn out for the best: he became Head Boy at Hayesbrook Secondary school, then he studied for his "A" Levels at West Kent College, which enabled him to go on to Loughbough University, where in 1989 he obtained a BSc (Hons) degree.

A reception was being held one evening at Langton House and after Pauline and I had finished our day's work we helped prepare the food. Then we made the punch. We added all manner of things — fruit and mint, as well as the alcohol. Of course, it had to be tasted so we could get it right and we were quite merry by the time the guests arrived. Jamie, the chauffeur, was waiting on the guests; he offered a dignitary some strawberry gateau and it fell on to his (the dignitary's) lap. He took it very well, especially with Pauline's help to clear it up. In fact, what with Pauline's cheeky comments, I think he quite enjoyed that incident!

I always took Bob to work with me during all the school holidays, so he was still able to play with his friends. My employers always treated me and my family with respect and I, in return, held them in great esteem. Pauline and I were invited to Safia's wedding in July

1999, an occasion we enjoyed very much. It was lovely to see the family again, especially Mrs Kashfi Shah. Sadly her husband, Idries Shah, had died in 1996. Working at Langton House changed me and my whole philosophy of life. It was not anything specific that was said to me, just the placid attitude and outlook they had there. They were the biggest influence of my later life. Idries Shah always believed in a good education but he said that most knowledge and experience came from learning from a master — like an apprenticeship, you see.

While working there I met Greville, another member of staff, whose duties included making furniture and chauffeuring. Greville had a talent for theatre work and had always wanted to go into the acting profession, but his middle-class parents would not allow it. Acting was still rather frowned upon by some people in those days. He had been a social worker instead, but his job had become too much for him when he realised that most of the people he worked with would not accept his help; it was too difficult for them to change the way they lived. He was very clever and artistic and that was how he came to work at Langton. He had a drink problem and we could see he was behaving strangely, but we didn't realise quite how ill he was. My employer asked if Ted and I would visit Greville at his home at the weekend just to see how he was, but we didn't go in the end because we heard his fiancée was going to stay with him that weekend. When I arrived at work the following Monday, I was told he had had a breakdown and been sectioned for 28 days. They said I shouldn't visit him as it would just be upsetting, but Ted and I did go to see him in the local institution. We had great problems finding his ward and were there for ages walking around in all directions. I think the patients must have spent their time turning the signs around. We were getting so frustrated that after a while Ted said, "So this is how they get their patients!" When we did find Greville he was so pleased to see us. It was not as frightening as we thought it would be. It must be awful to know you are mentally unwell and without friends.

On Greville's release he went home to Worthing to stay with his widowed mother for a while and eventually he returned to work. But his drinking became progressively worse and in due course he had another breakdown, this time while he was staying in Oxford. At that time I became quite friendly with his mother. She was so sad; her other two sons were abroad — one in the USA and one in Canada — and her husband had died a few years earlier, so she was having to cope all alone. Her husband had been a doctor and she used to say, "If only he were here, he would know what to do." Greville went home to his mother again after this second breakdown and got a job locally. His drinking caused his mother a good deal of worry and she used to tell him this. One day he threw himself out of the upstairs window. He broke his leg but was otherwise unhurt. After hospital treatment he went back to stay with his mother again, but it was all getting too much for her; she had a stroke and died a few days later. Greville's fiancée told him at this time that she could not marry him. The doctors put him under heavy sedation and he came to stay with us until things were sorted out — his mother's house was to be sold and he was to go and live with his brother in the United States. We took him to the airport, no problem; he was still on strong medication. But not long after, he returned to England. His illness had been diagnosed as manic depression. His return to us I shall never forget. John and Yvonne had quite a shock when they met him at Gatwick airport. He was very high and they had difficulty driving home with him. Our shock was even worse, because he was now going to live with us until he found a home of his own.

What a time we had! Eventually I heard of a caravan park in north Tonbridge where he could buy a caravan and have it all to himself. We duly smartened him up and he went and chose one, but it was about three months until he could move in — it was a new site and each stage of the development had to be passed by the council. In all, it was six months of sheer hell. Bob was studying for "A" levels then and Gerald was working irregular hours on the railway. We also had another lad staying — his father had come and asked me if his son could come and stay for a while as he was leaving the district. Graham — the son — and his father never got on. Graham had money problems and could not resist gambling but he always paid me regularly, although I think he borrowed from many people to do it. I had more trouble with Greville and Graham than I ever did with my four sons. After a while I had just about reached the end of my tether with Graham and felt we would have to ask him to leave, when my husband came up to my bedroom with a cup of tea one morning and said, "We've visitors downstairs." This lad had stayed out all night with his girlfriend and had come to tell us he was going to live with her parents; what a relief! They did actually marry. She is a very nice girl and she had a stabilising effect on him. Despite his problems he had always been polite and had a loving disposition.

Soon Greville was able to move into his mobile home. He began to do voluntary work at the local Oast Theatre, making scenery and masks, as well as doing some acting. At last he had found work he enjoyed. He had another two breakdowns after that but he always managed to get back in the theatre. He came to see us once a week for a meal and a chat and became part of the family for all the family gatherings, like birthdays and Christmas. He did not have many friends due to his illness but Neil, Lucinda, Richard, Helen and Helena remained faithful.

1983

Greville's brother Barry invited Ted and me to visit him and his wife Edite at their home in America; we were very excited. It was an interesting visit. We spent one day in New York; they lived only about 50 miles north of it. Rodney, Barry's son, escorted us on a tour of that great city. We were warned before leaving home not to take any valuables with us because Rodney had had a bad experience the previous week. While he was in New York all his money and credit cards were stolen from him at knifepoint. Fortunately, he knew people there who could help him. You can imagine how I felt, having heard all this, when we were running to catch the ferry to see Staten Island and the Statue of Liberty — the men were ahead of me, as I was wearing high-heeled shoes and so was slower and, suddenly, I felt a strong hand grip my shoulder. I turned and looked up into the face of a six-foot-tall black fellow and my heart was thumping in my chest; I thought, "This is it." But instead, the man was grinning from ear to ear. It turned out that my postcards had been falling out of my bag as I ran and he had been picking them up for me. He said, with this big grin, "Here you are, mam, I've been trying to catch you up." So, you see, it's not all bad in New York.

Next day we went by coach to Washington, DC. We visited Arlington National Cemetery and saw the graves of Jack and Robert Kennedy. The trees were in full bloom; the blossom was pale pink and looked lovely. Then we went to Mount Vernon, the home of George Washington, which was by the Potomac River. We visited Ford's Theatre, where Abraham Lincoln was assassinated, and also the house and bedroom where he is supposed to have actually died. We then visited the Capitol Building and Smithsonian Institute National Air and Space Museum. We saw the Apollo 11 space capsule, the crew's living quarters, the moon buggy and Gemini Space Shuttle, absolutely in awe of all we saw. I hope you too will have this experience one day. We also took our seats in the House of Representatives. The most exciting part of our trip was the visit to the White House. President Reagan was in office at that time. While we were queuing to go in, we saw a gardener digging up tulip bulbs. I asked if I could have a couple and he said, "Yes, mam," and gave me about half-a-dozen. I put them — all muddy — in my handbag. I still have them; they are blooming beautifully at the moment. I am doubly thrilled with them because when we arrived back at Barry's house the next day we learnt that our second grandson, David, had been born on that day. David will be 18 years old this week (2001), so I know they have bloomed every year for 18 years. I look at them and think of our visit to the White House and the House of Representatives.

In 1977 I left my employment at Langton Green and about a year later I got a job at CAF, a charity, working as a receptionist. There was a lot of excitement when it was announced that the Duke of Edinburgh was going to visit our offices. We were duly given instructions on where we had to stand, with various members of staff at strategic points to be introduced to him. My other humble colleagues and I, who were all the way down the pecking order, were told to stand demurely in a corner. When the Duke arrived, though, what do you think he did? He came straight over to where we were standing and spoke to us. He has the loveliest of blue eyes, I remember. I have a photo that was taken at that time; I look like a terrified rabbit, which indeed is what I felt like. Not because of him, I enjoyed meeting him, but because of the reaction of our manager. She was not pleased!

I had quite a good social life while I worked there. I retired on my 60th birthday and returned as a temp the following Monday, staying on in that capacity for several years. I made many friends there and even now we have a "wrinklies" lunch each year at the new office at King's Hill. Going back and meeting everybody is always very enjoyable.

Gerald married a nice girl, Jenny. Later she was expecting twins and there was great excitement in my department when Gerald rang the office to say that the babies were on their way. Eventually they arrived and we could all get on with our work! They were two beautiful boys and the doctor remarked that one day they would be six-footers. True to his word, they are — at 16 (2001). I hope they have stopped growing!

1986

Ted and I thought it was time to move to a smaller place. We found a very nice flat in the centre of town. We have been very happy here with Ted enjoying his retirement, either tinkering with his car or doing his joinery hobby in the garage, then going off to golf a couple of days a week.

At about this time I heard from a receptionist friend of mine that help was needed at the local baby clinic. I offered my services for just keeping the register and I went to help on Monday afternoons. I did this for many years. I found it to be most enlightening in modern baby care, so different from my experience of bringing up a baby. At this time more grandchildren were beginning to arrive for us, so I did not frown at baby being changed on a changing table. (I always had my babies on my lap for bathing, dressing, etc.) I never did get the hang of using a table or floor; seeing the modern methods was strange. No more terry nappies — it is disposables now. Also, dummies are very popular nowadays. I must admit that all the babies were happy and flourishing well, so modern methods probably are better.

I was also amazed at the clothes babies now wore and the bright colours. There was one eight-week-old baby wearing denim trousers, another with a peaked cap. We always had "Chilpruf" vests and clothes made from Vyella, so soft for baby's tender skin. The babies soon grew to toddlers. Then they came proudly to show me their new brother or sister. They also kept me busy at times.

Fathers also came with their wives, or even on their own, bringing baby for its check-up, undressing and dressing the tiny mites. They were so gentle with them — this was a real eye-opener to me. All in all it helped me to modernise my way of thinking.

1994

Our 50th wedding anniversary came on the 11th June, 1994. Our son Christopher came over from Germany bringing his wife and new baby, Sebastian, our eighth grandchild. We were very proud of our grandchildren: seven grandsons and just one granddaughter, our very dear Sarah Jane. Bob came too, bringing his current girlfriend. My sister had come down a few weeks earlier and persuaded me to have a new dress and Ted to get a new blazer, because we were being taken out to a posh restaurant by the family. We had expected one of our relatives to drive us there, but it turned out quite different — a white wedding car with white ribbons arrived to take us. The driver handed me an orchid to wear and gave Ted a carnation buttonhole. We were taken to the posh restaurant to find about 96 people there, including my bridesmaids; people who had been present at our marriage and we had not seen since then; relatives from far and wide including our eldest grandson and Anneleise, whom we had not seen for many years; friends and work colleagues. My daughter-in-law had spent two years organising this party with the help of other family members and friends. She also wrote a beautiful poem, which summed up our 50 years in a moving and vivid way.

On the 11th June 1944
towards the end of the Second World War
a handsome young couple called Peggy and Ted
went to Holy Cross Church to get themselves wed

The war all around them raged on at full tilt
while Peggy and Ted, dressed up to the hilt
walked down the aisle and solemnly vowed
and Ted's worldly goods to Peg he endowed

And so on that day they became Man and Wife
to love and cherish for the rest of their life
as they walked from the Church there rang not a bell
only of invasion their ringing would tell

The reception took place, Ted bought a barrel
but it was just after D-Day and no-one could travel
so, few people came to wish them the best
but at least there was plenty of beer for the rest

Down the road their first night was spent
at the home of a neighbour, kindly lent
there they spent their first night of passion
it was one of the few things that wasn't on ration

The honeymoon ended the very next day
when back to his unit Ted made his way

to continue the fight for more than a year
till at last they heard the final "all clear"

Now the war was over, life became humdrum
both working hard and living with Peg's mum
and soon their happiness was complete
when they heard the patter of Chris' tiny feet

At last they managed to get their own place
all to themselves it felt like a palace
then in nineteen fifty-two
the stork came again with son number two

Peggy said "right no more babies for me"
but in fifty-six came son number three
"that's it now" she thought "definitely no more"
but fate still had some surprises in store

When she found she was preggers she felt quite forlorn
but her gloom turned to joy when our Bobby was born
he was such a sweet little, dear little tot
just look at him now he's changed such a lot

They moved to Tonbridge in sixty-seven
to own their own home it felt like Heaven
the kids filled the house with laughter and noise
and saxophones, violins, pianos and toys

There were lodgers and students and friends
dropping round
all sure that a welcome there, would be found

Bob, John and Gerald all having rows
and hosepipe fights in and out of the windows

Now the boys have all up and grown
where has time gone it's surely flown
but you're still together after all these years
of happiness and laughter and just a few tears

Fifty years have passed since that day
and I think it would be fair to say
that ups and downs there have been few
and never a cross word . . . well perhaps one or two

Tonight Mum and Dad is just a token
of the Love that we feel, though it's seldom spoken
we drink to your health and happiness
and we thank you for everything, God Bless

How they managed to keep it all from us I will never know. It is a good thing they kept it from Ted; he would have had a migraine on the day if he had known. I wouldn't have had a migraine but it was better to have it as a surprise anyway, it was just unbelievable. I have a recorded tape of the whole evening and I occasionally look at it when I am feeling sorry for myself. In a strange way, it makes me feel at peace — knowing how fortunate we were to have such a wonderful family and great friends.

1995

In 1995, Greville died; he had a heart attack just outside the house where he used to live with us. His brother and two sisters-in-law came over for the funeral. Some neighbours of ours let them have the use of their furnished flat, which was unoccupied at the time.

We had a young neighbour, Paul, who was in the process of changing his career and spent long periods of time at home. He and Ted became very friendly; therefore Paul was of considerable help to me when Ted's health began to deteriorate. My friend Angela also helped me a great deal at that sad time.

Because of Ted's health, our family again came over from Germany to spend Christmas with us. We also celebrated our grandsons' second birthday. The neighbours once again kindly lent us their flat, so we were able to fit everyone in.

1996

It was very sad for me to lose Ted the following spring; we had known each other for 57 years. Of course we had arguments; I was always being told, "Don't nag, woman!" There was a funny incident once when I got very cross with my husband and sons. I was yelling and shouting at them and they were taking no notice. So I rushed out of the house, picking up my handbag on my way. I slammed the front door very hard and walked down to the station, hoping one of them would follow and ask me to come home. But none of them did. Then I discovered I had not got my purse or my door key. It was a very cold night, so all I could do was go back and ask to come in. There they were, all grinning; they had found my purse and knew I wouldn't have got far.

I still miss Ted and would very much like to have the old days back again, but of course that can never be. I visit my family as much as I can these days; I do not mind travelling alone but it can have its hazards — due mainly to the attitudes of travel agents and railway and airport staff. All seem incapable of giving correct information!

In June 2001 I visited my eldest grandson, Steven, in Dresden; he has a partner called Connie and he is the stepfather to her four sons. He is very happy with them all. I enjoyed my visit to them; I am well used to boys. Dresden is so very interesting and I would love to go there again someday. I also visited Frankfurt and stayed with Anneleise and her new partner, Larry, for a few days. My friend Angela came with me on the trip. She is good company with a great sense of cockney humour and fitted in with the families very well. We had plenty of amusing moments during that holiday. In September I went off to Scotland with John and Sylvia — you see, I keep quite busy and love travelling around. I am still bored with housework but it has to be done.

Angela was a good friend to me at that time. I miss her now that she is living on the Isle of Wight but I do visit her as often as I can.

1999

Bob is now living in Bath. He too is very fond of music. He learnt the violin for a time, but with all the pressures of studying he gave that up. He is doing very well and is a good son to me — he has given all his old computer equipment to me, for one thing and I am trying to learn how to use it. I go for lessons but I find it difficult to remember all I am told — that's because of old age, I suspect. Also he encouraged me to go for art classes, which I also find difficult, but it has taught me to look at everything differently, especially scenery. I often think I would like to paint this, that or the other; but of course I usually don't. I prefer pastels to watercolour; it is a bit easier.

2002

Gerald has been studying complementary medicine and has passed courses in reflexology, massage, Indian head massage and aromatherapy. We are proud. He can now display "MICHT.TATh.IIHHT" after his name!

John's eldest son, David, is now at Plymouth University. My grandsons, Mark, Stuart and Iain, are all studying hard at their various subjects too. My granddaughter, Sarah, is at the moment enjoying life; her hard work will start in a couple of years. At present her main interests are music and singing, but she would like to become a vet one day. Jamie is the sportsman of the family; his interest lies in football. Our eldest grandson, Steven, is a stonemason — he has passed his exams and now holds his master's ticket. He still lives in Dresden and has worked on the rebuilding of that beautiful city. Last but not least, young Sebastian. He too lives in Germany, in the Black Forest area and I am told he is a good swimmer and enjoys diving. I watched him diving and swimming under water last year. He is also learning the trumpet; I hope he will play for me when I next see him.

Our gracious Queen Mum died this year at 101 years old. I went with Jenny to pay my respects to her while she was lying in state in Westminster Hall. I had a sore heel at the time and was using a walking stick. When we reached Westminster Station we were amazed at the length of the queue. I asked a policeman if there was anywhere that I could sit down, as I was in great pain. He suggested I should speak to a policeman on duty nearer the entrance and he kindly directed us through to a courtyard where I could sit down. There was also a book of condolences, which Jenny and I were able to sign. Then we were conducted straight into the hall. I cannot describe what I felt when I saw her crown, her daughter's white wreath, the purple drapes of the catafalque against the gold carpeting and all the beauty of that hall. I shall never forget it. Afterwards we walked to St James's Park, by which time I was desperate for a sit down. After we had had something to eat and drink we decided we would try to walk to see the flowers outside Clarence House. We had to walk right up to Buckingham Palace and there were able to read the announcement which was hung on the railings of the palace. We saw all her floral tributes and then walked past the Queen's Chapel and St James's Palace; all in all, it was a wonderful goodbye to Her Majesty. I did not appreciate the long walk back along Pall Mall to catch our train home, but upon reflection, it was worth it.

Anneleise and Larry came for a visit in August and, surprisingly, the weather was great. After they had returned to Germany, Christopher brought Sebastian over. They explored Tonbridge Castle and spent a happy afternoon boating on the Medway. One day we all went off to London, had a trip down the Thames to visit HMS *Belfast* and then walked over Tower Bridge to see the Tower of London and the Crown Jewels. Next we caught a double-decker bus — Sebastian wanted to sit up at the top but I remained downstairs — to Whitehall to see the soldiers on horseback. It was rather late by then, but we saw the changing of the guard, when the horses and riders were dismissed to be replaced by foot soldiers — who seemed to me to be very young girls! I just stood in disbelief! We arrived home extremely tired, only to get up early the next morning to go to Portsmouth and visit Nelson's ship, HMS *Victory*. We did a trip round the harbour and saw HMS *Ark Royal* leaving to go on manoeuvres in the Middle East. We stayed in Southsea where Chris and Sebastian were able to have a good swim in the sea. Next day, Angela came over from the Isle of Wight and we all took the ferry to Gosport. The lads went off to visit the submarine berthed there, while Angela and I enjoyed a good gossip.

Soon after, I was off on a trip to the Black Forest. And what next? Well, Christmas with Gerald and Jenny and New Year with John and Yvonne . . .

I know we should not be always looking back, but I thought you young ones might be interested to know just how different our lives were from your own. My reflections have made me realise how the war and all the sacrifices that were made have given me the freedom to enjoy my old age. I have my own home, am independent and live in comparative luxury.

I hope you all have as interesting a life as I have had. There have been some low points, but they have just made me appreciate the good times all the more. I hope you have found these memories interesting and amusing and that they have shown how much our culture has changed with the passing of the years.

I could go on endlessly, chatterbox that I am.

Also available in ISIS Large Print:

Diary of a Lollipop Lady

Hazel Wheeler

"No wonder people weren't rushing to be crossing wardens, I thought ruefully next morning, a foggy first of February."

In February 1966, beset with money troubles and with a young family, Hazel Wheeler began work as a Lollipop Lady at the princely wage of £3 14s 6d a week. During her year spent shepherding schoolchildren over the crossing, she met many new people, young and old, and heard all about the ups and downs of their daily lives.

Hazel recorded her own experiences, together with the varying fortunes of her own family, in her diary, which forms the basis for this delightful and faithful memoir of her time on the "Lollipop Beat".

ISBN 978-0-7531-9392-1 (hb)
ISBN 978-0-7531-9393-8 (pb)

Before the Last All Clear

Ray Evans

"Except for Mam and Dad, none of us had ever been out of Liverpool before, never mind on a train."

This is the story of one young boy from Liverpool, whose family was sent to the Welsh town of Llanelli for the duration of the war. Separated from his mother, and brothers and sisters, six-year-old Raymond Evans was shunted form pillar to post. At first he had a miserable time, unwanted and largely unloved, and it appeared that his war would be spent without any family — real or surrogate. Ray's world is one of ration books, black-out curtains, air-raid sirens and sudden death; a world in which humanity triumphs despite its own shortcomings.

ISBN 978-0-7531-9380-8 (hb)
ISBN 978-0-7531-9381-5 (pb)

Children of Bethnal Green

Doris M. Bailey

"Dad loved me because I was bright and Mum because I was such a good-tempered baby."

Bethnal Green is at the heart of London's East End, infamous as the stamping ground of gangland bosses the Kray twins. But Doris Bailey recalls the humanity of Bethnal Green's back streets during the 1920s, 1930s and throughout the Second World War. She vividly remembers the endless struggle to make ends meet, the little shops and the people who ran them, the street sellers, and the very different world of Sunday School and chapel.

ISBN 978-0-7531-9378-5 (hb)
ISBN 978-0-7531-9379-2 (pb)

Country Boy

Colin Miller

"My childhood, especially during and soon after the war, was a delightful experience that I look back on with great affection and all of my family, not just my parents, made that possible."

Colin Miller was born in 1940 in Rollesby, a village near Great Yarmouth. In Rollesby, as in so many other rural communities at this time, drinking water was drawn from a well, the lavatory was a bucket in an outside privy, transport was a bicycle or a bus, and entertainment was provided by the radio, whist drives at the village hall or a rare visit to the cinema. As the 1940s and '50s progressed, this way of life changed dramatically — some would say disappeared. Colin Miller chronicles these developments through the eyes of a Norfolk schoolboy and teenager.

ISBN 978-0-7531-9358-7 (hb)
ISBN 978-0-7531-9359-4 (pb)

The Way We Were

Toni Savage

"Everything had two alternatives for us. The season was either summer or winter. The days were either good or bad. There was out or in. Out was most of the time."

An only child, Toni Savage was evacuated from London in September 1939. She was to spend over four years in the Surrey countryside, living in a country mansion with seven other children, under the watchful eyes of Mrs Parrot, Miss Bailey and the governess Mrs Samuel.

Although her life as an evacuee was often one of fun and laughter, full of new friends and the wonders of childhood, it was also lived in the shadow of the war, with both bombs and soldiers a common sight.

ISBN 978-0-7531-9344-0 (hb)
ISBN 978-0-7531-9345-7 (pb)

ISIS publish a wide range of books in large print, from fiction to biography. Any suggestions for books you would like to see in large print or audio are always welcome. Please send to the Editorial Department at:

ISIS Publishing Limited
7 Centremead
Osney Mead
Oxford OX2 0ES

A full list of titles is available free of charge from:

Ulverscroft Large Print Books Limited

(UK)
The Green
Bradgate Road, Anstey
Leicester LE7 7FU
Tel: (0116) 236 4325

(Australia)
P.O. Box 314
St Leonards
NSW 1590
Tel: (02) 9436 2622

(USA)
P.O. Box 1230
West Seneca
N.Y. 14224-1230
Tel: (716) 674 4270

(Canada)
P.O. Box 80038
Burlington
Ontario L7L 6B1
Tel: (905) 637 8734

(New Zealand)
P.O. Box 456
Feilding
Tel: (06) 323 6828

Details of ISIS complete and unabridged audio books are also available from these offices. Alternatively, contact your local library for details of their collection of ISIS large print and unabridged audio books.